CW00828943

MARK O'ROWE

Mark O'Rowe is a writer and director.

His plays include *From Both Hips* (Fishamble Theatre Company), *Howie the Rookie* (Bush Theatre), *Made in China* (Peacock Theatre), *Crestfall* (Gate Theatre), *Terminus* (Peacock Theatre), *Our Few and Evil Days* (Abbey Theatre) and *The Approach* (Landmark Productions).

He has also adapted several works, including Ibsen's *Hedda Gabler* (Abbey Theatre), *DruidShakespeare*, an amalgamation of four of Shakespeare's history plays (Druid Theatre Company), and Ibsen's *Ghosts* (a Landmark/Abbey Theatre co-production).

Screenplays include *Intermission*, *Boy A*, *Perrier's Bounty*, *Broken* and *The Delinquent Season,* which he also directed.

TV includes the series *Temple* and *Normal People*.

Mark O'Rowe

REUNION

NICK HERN BOOKS
London
www.nickhernbooks.co.uk

A Nick Hern Book

Reunion first published in Great Britain in 2024 as a paperback original by Nick Hern Books Limited, The Glasshouse, 49a Goldhawk Road, London W12 8QP, in association with Landmark Productions and Galway International Arts Festival

Reunion copyright © 2024 Mark O'Rowe

Mark O'Rowe has asserted his moral right to be identified as the author of this work

Cover photograph by Kris Askey

Designed and typeset by Nick Hern Books, London
Printed in Great Britain by Mimeo Ltd, Huntingdon, Cambridgeshire PE29 6XX

A CIP catalogue record for this book is available from the British Library

ISBN 978 1 83904 378 9

www.nickhernbooks.co.uk/environmental-policy

Reunion was first performed at the Black Box Theatre as part of the Galway International Arts Festival on 15 July 2024. The cast, in order of appearance, was as follows:

ELAINE	Cathy Belton
FELIX	Stephen Brennan
MARILYN	Valene Kane
HOLLY	Simone Collins
CIARAN	Leonard Buckley
MAURICE	Robert Sheehan
GINA	Catherine Walker
JANICE	Venetia Bowe
STUART	Desmond Eastwood
AONGHUS	Ian-Lloyd Anderson

Director	Mark O'Rowe
Set Designer	Francis O'Connor
Lighting Designer	Sinéad McKenna
Sound Designer	Aoife Kavanagh

Production Manager	Jim McConnell
Stage Manager	Brendan Galvin
Assistant Stage Manager	Ciara Gallagher
Hair and Make-up	Tee Elliott
Fight Director	Ciaran O'Grady
Costume Supervisor	Nicola Burke
Sound Engineer	Mike Nestor
Scenic Artist	Sandra Butler
Chief LX	Susan Collins
Carpenter	Martin Wallace
Crew	Danny Hones, Gus McDonagh
Set Construction	TPS

Producers	Anne Clarke I Landmark
	Paul Fahy I GIAF
Associate Producer	Jack Farrell I Landmark
Marketing	Sinead McPhillips
Publicity	Sinead O'Doherty I O'Doherty Communications
Photographers	Production I Marcin Lewandowski
	Rehearsal I Shane O'Connor
	Publicity image I Kris Askey
Videography	Gansee
Graphic Design	Gareth Jones
	Hilda Reid I Wish Design Solutions

Landmark Productions

Landmark Productions is one of Ireland's leading theatre producers. It produces wide-ranging work in Ireland and shares that work with international audiences.

Led by Anne Clarke since the company's foundation in 2004, its productions have received multiple awards and have been seen in leading theatres in London, New York and beyond.

It co-produces regularly with a number of partners, including, most significantly, Galway International Arts Festival, Irish National Opera and the Abbey Theatre. Its 30 world premieres – and counting – include new plays by major Irish writers such as Mark O'Rowe, Enda Walsh, Marina Carr and Deirdre Kinahan, featuring a roll-call of Ireland's finest actors, directors and designers.

Numerous awards include the Judges' Special Award at the Irish Times Irish Theatre Awards, in recognition of 'sustained excellence in programming and for developing imaginative partnerships to bring quality theatre to the Irish and international stage'; and a Special Tribute Award for Anne Clarke, for her work as 'a producer of world-class theatre in the independent sector in Ireland'.

In January 2021 it established Landmark Live, a new online streaming platform which enables it to bring the thrill of live theatre to audiences around the world.

Producer	Anne Clarke
Associate Producer	Jack Farrell
Marketing Manager	Sinead McPhillips
Publicity	Sinead O'Doherty | O'Doherty Communications

landmarkproductions.ie
X/LandmarkIreland
Facebook.com/landmarkireland
Instagram/landmarkireland

Galway International Arts Festival

Galway International Arts Festival is a major cultural organisation, which produces one of Europe's leading international arts festivals; develops and produces new work that tours nationally and internationally; and presents a major discussion platform, First Thought Talks. The Festival takes place each July in Galway, Ireland with attendances in excess of 400,000.

The Festival tours its own productions and exhibitions nationally and internationally, and with its co-producing partners has recently toured to London, New York, Edinburgh, Chicago, Washington, Adelaide and Sydney.

The Festival commissioned and produced John Gerrard's *Mirror Pavilion* during Galway European Capital of Culture 2020 which following its premiere in Galway toured to the Gwanjgu Biennale, South Korea 2021 and Sydney Biennale Spring 2022.

Other notable productions include *Misterman*, *Ballyturk* [Best Production at the Irish Theatre Awards], *Arlington* and *Medicine* [Galway, Edinburgh Festival, New York 2021], all by Enda Walsh [all co-produced with Landmark Productions]; and *Incantata* by Paul Muldoon which toured to New York in 2020. The Festival's productions of the immersive theatre installation series *Rooms*, created by Enda Walsh and Paul Fahy, have toured to New York, Washington and London.

Galway International Arts Festival would like to acknowledge the support of its principal funding agencies the Arts Council and Fáilte Ireland; its Drinks Partner Heineken; and Education Partner University of Galway.

Chief Executive	John Crumlish
Artistic Director	Paul Fahy
Financial Controller	Gerry Cleary
Communications and Development Manager	Hilary Martyn
Administrator	Jacinta Dwyer
Marketing Manager	Tracey Ferguson
Head of Production	Adam Fitzsimons
Fundraising Manager	Aisling O'Sullivan
Digital Media Manager	Mary McGraw
Volunteers and EDI Manager	Elena Toniato

giaf.ie
X/GalwayIntArts
Facebook.com/GalwayInternationalArtsFest
Instagram/galwayintarts

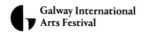

For my dad

Characters

ELAINE
GINA, *Elaine's sister*
JANICE, *Elaine's daughter*
MARILYN, *Elaine's daughter*
MAURICE, *Elaine's son*
STUART, *Janice's partner*
CIARAN, *Marilyn's partner*
HOLLY, *Maurice's partner*
FELIX, *Holly's father*
AONGHUS, *Marilyn's ex*

Setting

The kitchen / living room of a house on an island off the coast of Ireland.

Front door, a large window, exit left, exit right, stairs.

This text went to press before the end of rehearsals and so may differ slightly from the play as performed.

ACT ONE

ELAINE *peels potatoes over the sink.* MARILYN *stands at the window, looking out.*

FELIX *enters from outside.*

ELAINE. All right, Felix?

FELIX. Yeah, do you mind if I get another beer?

ELAINE. Of course not.

He goes to the fridge and gets one.

FELIX. Pretty wild out there.

ELAINE. Sorry?

FELIX. The water. Pretty choppy.

ELAINE. Right.

Beat. He exits again. Beat.

MARILYN. It is.

ELAINE. Huh?

MARILYN. It *is* pretty choppy. (*Beat.*) Come over and have a look. (*Beat.*) Ma.

ELAINE *sighs, then joins her at the window.*

Look at the height of those there!

ELAINE. Jesus. (*Long pause.*) Would you say they'll cancel the ferry?

MARILYN. Ah, yeah. You couldn't let people cross in *those* kinds of conditions.

ELAINE. I suppose.

Beat. She returns to the sink and resumes peeling. After a moment:

I hate when there's someone who doesn't fit in.

MARILYN. Felix?

ELAINE. Yeah.

MARILYN. No, I know what you mean. You're always worrying if they're okay...

ELAINE. Exactly.

MARILYN.... if they're feeling left out or whatever... (*Beat; then, turning away from the window.*) Can *I* do something?

ELAINE. No.

MARILYN. Are you sure? You don't have to be the *martyr*, now.

ELAINE. I'm not *being* the martyr. Put these skins in the bucket, then.

MARILYN. *What?!* I'm messing.

She starts moving potato skins from the sink to a bucket. HOLLY *enters from upstairs.*

ELAINE. Well?

HOLLY. No.

MARILYN. You can use *mine*, Holly.

HOLLY. Ah, sure we'll see if Maurice has any luck.

ELAINE. Is your da all right, Holly?

HOLLY. What do you mean?

ELAINE. No, I'm just saying, he's welcome to hang out with us in *here*.

HOLLY. He's fine.

ELAINE. Are you sure?

HOLLY. Yeah, no, there's nothing he'd rather now than what he's doing. Sit with his beer...

MARILYN. Right.

HOLLY.... looking out at the sea...

MARILYN. There's tea there, Holly.

HOLLY. Hm? Oh, cool. (*Going to the table.*) No, he's grand, Elaine.

ELAINE. Okay.

She continues to peel the potatoes. HOLLY *pours herself a cup of tea, sits down, takes a sip. Pause.*

HOLLY. So, what was the story with Janice and Stuart?

ELAINE. Agh. His mother was meant to mind the kids, but then the dates conflicted with a trip she wanted to go on...

MARILYN. A hiking trip.

ELAINE. Is that what it was?

HOLLY. And would they not have just *brought* them?

ELAINE. I think it's a break from them they were *looking* for.

HOLLY. Okay...

CIARAN (*offstage; from outside*). Hey, Felix.

MAURICE (*offstage; from outside*). All right, Felix?

FELIX (*offstage*). Lads.

HOLLY (*to* ELAINE)....but if they're stuck with them now in *any* case...

ELAINE. Hm? I know.

HOLLY....then...

ELAINE. Listen: your guess is as good as mine, Holly. I'd love to have had them *all* here.

MAURICE (*as he and* CIARAN *enter from outside*). Who?

ELAINE. Janice and Stuart...

MAURICE. Oh, right.

ELAINE....the kids.

MAURICE. Is your da okay out there, Holly?

HOLLY. Yeah, he's fine.

MAURICE (*of* ELAINE *and* MARILYN). And have they been abusing you?

ELAINE. What?!

MAURICE. I bet you you *have*.

HOLLY. They haven't.

MARILYN. And she can hold her own in *any* case. Right, Holly?

HOLLY. Exactly.

MAURICE. Right. Anyway…

He puts a plastic bag on the table. Then, taking each item out:

…bananas… cereal… biscuits… eggs…

ELAINE. They didn't have digestives?

MAURICE. No. *Or* Chef Sauce, so… (*Takes out a bottle of YR sauce.*)

ELAINE. Ah, no!

MARILYN. Ah, you're *joking*!

HOLLY. Did they have a charger?

MAURICE. You didn't *find* yours?

HOLLY. No.

MAURICE (*beat; then, taking one out of the bag*). Well then, you're lucky they *did*.

HOLLY. Oh, brilliant!

MARILYN (*of the bananas*). Can I have one of these?

MAURICE. No.

She picks one up and starts peeling it while HOLLY *plugs in her phone.*

MARILYN. Bit *obsessive* about your phone, Holly, are you?

HOLLY. Yeah, I suppose.

MAURICE. If it goes below sixty per cent, she gets very anxious.

HOLLY. It's like a security thing. *I* dunno…

MARILYN. Right.

HOLLY.... or an *in*security thing.

MAURICE. So, when are we eating, Ma?

ELAINE. Emm...

MARILYN. I'm *already* eating.

ELAINE.... say, around seven...?

MAURICE. Cool.

ELAINE.... half seven? (*To* CIARAN *and* HOLLY.) Is that okay for *you* guys?

CIARAN. Yeah, whenever.

HOLLY (*simultaneously*). Absolutely.

ELAINE (*beat*). Nice traditional dinner.

MAURICE. Exactly.

ELAINE. Bit of *chicken*...

MARILYN. Mmm.

ELAINE.... some roast *potatoes*...

HOLLY. I actually *love* YR sauce on roast potatoes.

ELAINE. Oh *really*!

HOLLY. Mm.

MAURICE. Well, *that* worked out well for you, *didn't* it.

MARILYN (*to* CIARAN). Did you call your folks?

CIARAN. I did, yeah.

MARILYN. And...?

CIARAN. Yeah, no, everything's fine.

ELAINE. Of course it is, Ciaran. And what do you think of the island?

MARILYN. They only went to the shop, Ma.

ELAINE. Well, what does he think of that *part* of the island.

CIARAN. Beautiful, yeah.

MAURICE (*to the women*). Did you see the waves?!

MARILYN. I know!

MAURICE. Bloody boat was like this! (*Demonstrates with his hand.*)

MARILYN. The ferry?!

CIARAN. Mm.

MARILYN. They didn't cancel it?

MAURICE. Would we have *seen* it if they'd cancelled it?

ELAINE. And was Sheila there, Maurice?

MAURICE (*to* HOLLY*, as he reaches for the teapot*). Anything left in this?

HOLLY. Yeah.

MAURICE (*picks it up*). There's isn't.

ELAINE. Maurice…

MAURICE. No, some other woman.

MARILYN (*to* CIARAN). Sheila had a thing for Maurice – (*To* MAURICE.) didn't she?

ELAINE. No, she didn't.

MARILYN. Well, she always gave him more *attention* than anyone else. 'A litre of milk, is it, Maurice…?'

MAURICE (*looking around*). Where's the, uh…?

MARILYN. '…A ride, is it, Maurice?'

ELAINE. A *what*?!

MARILYN. She was about a hundred, Holly.

MAURICE. Where are the teabags?

ELAINE (*gesturing to the counter*). There.

MAURICE. Ah, right.

MARILYN. Used to drive Janice mad. 'Why does *he* get special treatment?'

CIARAN. And would you never go anywhere else, Elaine?

ELAINE. On holidays?

CIARAN. Yeah.

ELAINE. Ah, once or *twice*, we did. But *here* was...

MARILYN. Absolutely.

ELAINE. ...*Wasn't* it.

MAURICE. Here was like a *tradition*, Ciaran.

MARILYN. Exactly.

HOLLY (*to* MARILYN). And what would you do?

MARILYN. For fun, like?

HOLLY. Yeah.

MARILYN. *I* dunno. Explore...

HOLLY. Uh-huh.

MARILYN. ...hang out with other kids... When we got older, we kind of hung out a lot *together*, didn't we.

ELAINE. Mm.

HOLLY. Just here?

MARILYN. Or in Lynch's.

HOLLY. Right.

ELAINE. ...or go for walks...

MARILYN. There's some beautiful walks, Holly.

HOLLY. Really?!

ELAINE. That reminds me, I need to air my runners out.

MARILYN. You need to buy a *new* bloody pair. (*To* MAURICE.) Have you *seen* her runners?

HOLLY. And are there beaches?

MARILYN. Yeah, but they're tiny.

HOLLY. Right.

MARILYN. *And* stony. Like you wouldn't be *sun*bathing on them or anything.

HOLLY. Can you swim?

MARILYN. Can *I* swim?

HOLLY. No, like...

MARILYN. Oh, can you *swim*. *Ah* yeah.

HOLLY. And *would* you?

ELAINE. When they were kids, they did.

MARILYN. Yeah, when we didn't *know* any better. It's freezing, Holly.

HOLLY. I don't mind the cold. What do you think, Maurice?

MAURICE. Hm?

HOLLY. Do you wanna come for a swim with me maybe tomorrow morning?

Pause.

MARILYN. Maurice, your girlfriend's asking you a question.

MAURICE. Yeah, if you want.

ELAINE. Jesus, you don't sound too *enthusiastic*, Maurice... Ah no, Marilyn!!

MARILYN. What?!

She is about to drop her banana skin into the bin.

Oh, right.

She throws it into the bucket instead. Then:

(*To* HOLLY.) For the birds tomorrow.

HOLLY. The *birds*?!

MAURICE. Ah, it's just something my da used to do.

ELAINE. He'd bring all the leftovers down to the turn in the mornings...

MAURICE. You know the turn, just...?

HOLLY. Yeah.

ELAINE. ...from the previous day, like, and dump them out on the rocks.

CIARAN. And would that be allowed?

ELAINE. 'Allowed'?!

CIARAN. You know, in terms of the natural habitat...

ELAINE. The...

CIARAN. ...interfering with it, or...

ELAINE. Oh. Well, nobody ever *said* it wasn't – (*To* MARILYN.) did they?

MAURICE. The amount that'd come, though...

ELAINE. They'll see sure.

MAURICE. ...in the space of what? Five minutes?

ELAINE. Less.

MARILYN. *Two* minutes.

MAURICE (*to* CIARAN *and* HOLLY). Sure youse'll see. Bloody *noise* of them.

HOLLY. Loud?

MAURICE. *Ah* yeah. (*Long pause.*) Weird being here without him, isn't it.

ELAINE. Mm. (*Long pause.*) Kinda like...

FELIX. Sorry, Elaine...? (*Beat; he is standing in the doorway.*) There's people.

ELAINE. *People!*

FELIX. Uh-huh.

ELAINE (*goes to the window*). Oh, my God!

MARILYN. Who is it?

ELAINE. Oh, my *God*!

She dashes outside.

MARILYN. Who is it?

MAURICE (*now at the window*). Gina!

MARILYN. *Gina?!*

MAURICE. And Janice and Stuart.

MARILYN. What?!

    MAURICE *exits*. MARILYN *goes to the window*.

ELAINE (*offstage; from outside*). Oh, my God!

GINA (*offstage*). Don't talk to me.

ELAINE (*offstage*). What the hell are you *doing* here?!

GINA (*offstage*). Did you see those waves?

MAURICE (*offstage*). Hey, Gina!

GINA (*offstage*). Hey, Maurice!

ELAINE (*offstage*). Come inside! Hey, love.

JANICE (*offstage*). Hey, Mam.

GINA (*offstage*). Did you *see* them?

ELAINE (*offstage*). Yeah.

GINA (*offstage*). And would having seen them not suggest that I now need something to calm my nerves?

ELAINE (*offstage*). Well, come in and we'll *give* you something.

    GINA *enters, carrying a travelling bag*.

MARILYN. Hey, Gina.

GINA. Hey, darling. (*Drops her bag inside the door, then hugs her.*) I'm bloody *trau*matised!

    ELAINE *and* MAURICE *enter, followed by* JANICE *and* STUART, *who also drop their bags just inside the door.*

ELAINE (*to* GINA). So you flew into… What did you…?

GINA. Flew into Dublin…

ELAINE. Okay.

GINA (*to* JANICE)....on Thursday, was it? (*To* ELAINE.) ...stayed with the guys...

ELAINE. So this was all, like, planned?

JANICE. Yeah.

ELAINE. As a surprise?

JANICE. Uh-huh.

ELAINE. You sneaky little bitch! (*To* STUART.) So what happened your mother's hiking thing? I can't believe this!

STUART. There *was* none.

ELAINE. What?!

STUART. Well there *was*, but...

ELAINE. *Ass*holes! (*To* GINA.) Oh my God, how *are* you?

GINA. How *am* I? I just had a near-death bloody experience.

MAURICE. It wasn't *that* bad, was it?

GINA. You've no idea, Maurice. Janice?

ELAINE. I'd say *you* were a gibbering wreck, were you, Janice?

JANICE. I wasn't far bloody *off* it...

GINA. Any sign of that drink, Elaine?

ELAINE. Oh sorry!

MAURICE. I'll get it. Whiskey, Gina?

GINA. Whatever.

JANICE....At first, like, everyone's out on the deck: 'Oh, isn't this exciting?!' Then two minutes later, we're all inside and everyone's really quiet...

GINA. That's right.

JANICE....no one's talking.

GINA. Well, everybody was making their peace. *I* certainly was.

JANICE (*of* STUART). This fella's laughing at us.

STUART. Well I just thought, if they haven't taken the life jackets out yet, then they mustn't be *too* concerned.

JANICE (*to* ELAINE). Were you on the eleven?

ELAINE. Yeah.

GINA. And what was *that* like?

ELAINE. Yeah, calm enough.

GINA. Of course it was.

JANICE. I dunno. I can't deny I found myself thinking about Abigail and Tom, who'd raise them…

STUART. You're joking!

MAURICE. Ah, Janice!

JANICE. No, I know, but these are the kinds of things that go through your head, you know?

GINA. They are. *I* was, like…

MARILYN. Who *would* you get to raise them?

ELAINE. Marilyn…!

MARILYN. Sorry, Gina.

GINA. You're grand. No, just, I was like, 'This is it…'

MAURICE. Uh-huh.

GINA. '…this is how you go.'

STUART. But if they hadn't even gotten the *life* jackets out…

GINA. Do you really think those savages care about protocol, Stuart?

ELAINE. Gina!

GINA. I'm joking… (*As he hands her a drink.*) Thanks, Maurice.

MAURICE. Janice?

JANICE. A glass of white wine, please, Maurice.

GINA. …or am I? Your man Padraig's still an ignorant fucker…

MAURICE. Stuart?

STUART. I'm grand.

GINA (*gruffly*)....'Get off that fucking thing!' (*To* JANICE.) Did you hear him?

JANICE. Yeah, no, I know.

GINA. I'd have hit him a fucking dig. (*Extending her hand to* HOLLY.) Hey. Gina.

HOLLY (*shaking it*). Holly.

GINA. Nice to meet you.

MARILYN. And this is Ciaran, Gina.

GINA. Oh, hi…

CIARAN. Hey.

GINA (*as they shake hands*)....Nice to meet you.

JANICE (*as he hands her a glass of white wine*). Thanks, Maurice.

GINA (*holding up her now empty glass*). And can I get another one of these, please, Maurice?

MAURICE (*taking it*). Sure.

ELAINE (*to* GINA)....And this is Holly's dad. Felix.

GINA. Oh, right. (*As they shake hands.*) Do you know, I actually thought, as we were arriving…

She stops.

JANICE What?

GINA. Ah, it doesn't matter.

MARILYN. Ah, don't say, 'It doesn't matter'!

GINA (*to* MAURICE, *who has just handed her another drink*). Thank you, Maurice.

She takes a sip; beat.

JANICE. *What* did you think?

GINA. No, just that your ma might have had a new *man* in her life.

MARILYN. Felix?!

ELAINE (*simultaneously*). Are you *joking*?! Jesus, that sounded horrible! Sorry, Felix.

FELIX. That's okay. Do you mind if I take another beer?

ELAINE. No, help yourself. That's what they're there for.

MAURICE (*to* STUART). So, did your mother just decide not to go, or what?

STUART. Where? Oh right, no, what happened was, a friend of hers in the group sprained her ankle getting off a bus, then her best friend decided...

MAURICE (*pouring himself a cup of tea*). Your mother's.

STUART. No, the woman who sprained her ankle's.

MAURICE. Oh, right.

STUART.... decided she wasn't gonna go either, and Mam doesn't really know the others very well, so...

ELAINE. Uh-huh.

STUART.... she thought she'd give this one a miss...

FELIX (*to* HOLLY; *gesturing outside*). I'm just gonna...

HOLLY. Yeah.

FELIX (*to* JANICE, STUART *and* GINA). Nice to meet you, guys.

GINA. You too, Felix.

JANICE.... which she may end up regretting.

STUART. Exactly.

ELAINE. Why?

JANICE. Ah, you know how tricky Tom can be.

ELAINE. He's not that bad.

GINA. He's *lovely*!

STUART. Yeah, I dunno. He seemed to be on his best behaviour while *you* were...

JANICE/MARILYN (*now that* FELIX *has gone outside*). *Ma-am!*

ELAINE. I'm so sorry, Holly.

HOLLY. That's okay.

ELAINE. Have I offended him?

HOLLY. Of *course* not, *God...*

GINA. That was *my* fault, actually.

HOLLY. Don't be silly...!

MAURICE (*teapot in hand*). Holly?

HOLLY. Yeah, please. (*To* GINA *and* ELAINE.) ...Seriously.

JANICE. So, are we in the corner room, Mam?

ELAINE. No, Holly and Maurice are in there.

JANICE (*beat*). Oh, right.

MARILYN. Well, you weren't *coming*, Janice.

JANICE. I know. No, it's fine, I just... It'll be weird not having it.

ELAINE. Well, why don't you swap?

MAURICE. Huh?

ELAINE. Why don't you swap? It's not as if there's much of a difference.

MAURICE. Well, the *view*, though.

ELAINE. Yeah, but does that make a difference?

MAURICE. Well then, why don't we *not* swap, so?

HOLLY. Ah Maurice...

MAURICE. What?

JANICE. Cos I'm used to the corner one.

HOLLY. ...she's used to the corner one.

MAURICE. She hasn't been here in five bloody *years*.

HOLLY (*beat; to* ELAINE). *I've* no problem switching.

MAURICE. Are you sure?

JANICE. Stuart?

STUART. Listen, I'm easy either way. As long as I get a pint in me soon.

JANICE. All right, great. I don't wanna be picky.

MARILYN. You *are* being picky.

ELAINE. Marilyn.

JANICE (*to* MAURICE). All right, well then, look: just stay where you are.

MAURICE. Janice…

JANICE. No, it's easier anyway.

MAURICE. *Janice*, you can have the room.

JANICE. All right, thanks.

ELAINE (*of* FELIX). I hope I haven't offended him.

JANICE. Who? Oh…

GINA. I doubt you did, Elaine.

HOLLY. She *didn't*! *God!*

GINA. He's quiet, is he, Holly?

HOLLY. Yeah.

MAURICE. He's been on his own the last few years, so we thought…

HOLLY. Well, *you* did.

MAURICE. *I* did. Sorry… that we might invite him, give him a taste of island living.

GINA. But he's single, you're saying.

HOLLY. Yeah.

GINA. Okay. Must make a note of that.

ELAINE. Ah, Gina…!

GINA. I'm messing!

ELAINE.….Jesus!

GINA (*pretending to call out the door*). I'm joking, Felix! (*To the others*.) He's probably running down to the ferry, is he?

STUART. So listen: who fancies a swift one?

ELAINE. I'm okay.

GINA. Me too.

STUART. Maurice?

MAURICE. Sure.

STUART. Ciaran?

CIARAN. Huh?

STUART. Do you want to head down to Lynch's?

MARILYN. Ah, yeah. The men go down to the pub while the women have to stay at home.

STUART. I just invited you!

MARILYN. Still, though.

STUART. What?

MARILYN. Nothing. Just it's very gender-typical behaviour.

STUART. Well, so is yours if you don't come with us.

MARILYN. No, you're all right.

MAURICE (*to* HOLLY). Do you wanna go?

HOLLY. No, but *you* go if you like.

MAURICE. Are you sure?

STUART. Janice?

JANICE. No, I'm okay.

ELAINE. Ask Felix.

STUART. Um... (*Beat.*) All right.

ELAINE (*to* GINA). I can't believe you're here!

GINA. Me neither.

STUART (*in the doorway*). Felix? Myself and the lads are going down to the pub, do you wanna come with us?

FELIX (*offstage*). No, that's okay.

STUART. Are you sure?

FELIX (*offstage*). Thanks for the offer, though.

STUART (*returning, to* ELAINE). He wants to stay.

MAURICE (*to* ELAINE). So, seven or half, you're saying.

ELAINE. Yeah, I'll give you a shout. Go easy, though, won't you?

JANICE. Exactly. Don't be making a show of yourselves.

MAURICE. 'A show of ourselves'! (*To* HOLLY.) Will you be okay?

HOLLY. Yeah, I'll be fine.

MAURICE (*of his mother and sisters*). Don't take any of their abuse.

ELAINE. *What* bloody abuse?!

JANICE. Bloody cheek of you!

MARILYN (*to* CIARAN). Here.

They kiss.

STUART (*to* JANICE). You remember the days?

JANICE. What days?

STUART. When you'd kiss at every parting.

JANICE. We kiss all the time!

STUART. I know.

He kisses her.

MAURICE. Jesus, well if *everyone's* fucking doing it...

He kisses HOLLY*; everyone laughs.*

STUART. Right. Come on.

CIARAN. See you later.

ELAINE. By-ee!

MARILYN (*simultaneously*). By-ee!

MAURICE, CIARAN *and* STUART *exit.*

MAURICE (*offstage*). See you later, Felix.

FELIX (*offstage*). Yeah, see you.

ELAINE (*after a moment, to* GINA). So. What made you decide to join us anyway?

GINA. Just taking advantage of my newfound freedom.

ELAINE. How are you?

GINA. I'm fine.

ELAINE. Are you sure?

JANICE. Gina broke up with her partner, Holly.

HOLLY. Oh, right…

MARILYN. You *what*?!

GINA. Yeah.

HOLLY.…sorry to hear that.

GINA. Thanks.

MARILYN. And when did *this* happen?

GINA. Couple of weeks ago. Three weeks?

MARILYN (*to* ELAINE). Did *you* know?

ELAINE. Yeah.

MARILYN. Why didn't you say?

ELAINE. Well, it was told in confidence, so…

MARILYN (*to* JANICE). And *you* knew.

JANICE. Well, obviously, since she's been staying with us…

MARILYN. And what happened? That's awful, Gina.

GINA. Yeah.

MARILYN. And what happened?

GINA. He left me.

MARILYN. He *left* you?! Why?

GINA. So he could sleep with other women.

MARILYN. Really?!

GINA. Well, more or less, yeah. He told me... (*To* HOLLY.)
   He'd just turned fifty, you see...

HOLLY. And how long had you been together?

GINA. Thirteen years?

HOLLY. Right.

GINA. And one night... I know. And one night he told me he
   wasn't ready yet to commit to only ever having sex with one
   person the rest of his life, so...

MARILYN. Is that what he actually *said*?!

GINA. Among other things, yeah.

MARILYN. Jesus.

GINA. ...said maybe a few years down the line our paths'd
   cross again, I said, 'Dave: if you're leaving me, you're
   leaving me.'

ELAINE. Exactly.

GINA. 'Forever. I won't be taking you back.' And he said,
   'Well, okay, then.'

MARILYN. Oh, I'm so sorry, Gina.

GINA. That's okay.

MARILYN. Are you devastated?

GINA. Do I *look* devastated?

MARILYN. No, but you could be putting on a brave face.

GINA. I suppose.

   Beat; she starts crying.

MARILYN. Oh, you *are*!

GINA. I'm okay.

MARILYN. Oh, you poor *thing*!

GINA. I'm okay. I'm fine.

ELAINE. Oh, Gina.

GINA. Stop. This kind of thing doesn't happen generally. And I *am* fine, I just...

ELAINE. I know.

GINA....it just kind of snuck up on me there for some reason. I'm actually *really happy*.

Beat. They laugh. FELIX *enters.*

HOLLY. All right, Dad?

FELIX (*to* ELAINE) Do you mind if I get another beer?

ELAINE. You don't have to *ask*, Felix.

FELIX (*goes to the fridge, gets one; beat*). Seems to be getting less choppy.

JANICE. Hm?

FELIX. The water.

GINA (*to* JANICE). Yeah, now that we've gone through hell!

JANICE. Exactly.

FELIX exits again. Pause.

So, do you mind if we move your stuff *now*, Holly?

HOLLY. Sorry?

JANICE. Out of my room.

MARILYN. Out of *your* room?

JANICE. Out of the corner room.

HOLLY. Sure.

MARILYN. What's your hurry?

JANICE. I wanna get *our* stuff *in*.

MARILYN. Sure get it in later.

JANICE. Yeah, but I don't *wanna* get it in later. I wanna relax now I'm here, and I won't be able to, knowing...

MARILYN. Fine.

HOLLY. No, that's fine. I'm happy to do it now.

GINA (*as* HOLLY *and* JANICE *grab Janice and Stuart's bags and head for the stairs*). Where am *I*?

ELAINE. Well, that's the thing: if I'd known you were *coming*...

JANICE. Yeah, but then you wouldn't have had your lovely surprise!

ELAINE (*to* GINA). Is downstairs all right?

GINA. I'm easy.

ELAINE. Well then, we'll put you down in that room beside the utility.

GINA. That little *parlour* room?

ELAINE. Yeah.

GINA *looks at her.*

Gina...

GINA. No, fine.

ELAINE. The couch converts to a bed, so...

GINA. No, that's cool.

JANICE *and* HOLLY *have now disappeared upstairs.*

MARILYN (*to* ELAINE). Do you *hear* her!

ELAINE. Marilyn...

MARILYN. No, but what does it *matter* what room she gets? 'I'm used to the corner one'!

ELAINE (*to* GINA, *holding her hand out across the table*). Good to see you, sis.

MARILYN.... Fucking unbelievable!

GINA (*taking* ELAINE*'s hand*). Good to see *you*.

ACT TWO

A few hours later. GINA, JANICE, MARILYN *and* HOLLY *sit around the table, while* ELAINE *stands at the counter putting food onto plates. Gina's bags are gone.*

ELAINE. Well, I was the oldest…

GINA. True.

ELAINE.…I had to make the mistakes while you just watched and learned from me what to do and what not to.

HOLLY. So who was the boldest?

ELAINE. Her.

GINA. Again, I was more clued in from watching *her*, and so I was far more, what would you say…?

JANICE. Sly.

ELAINE. Yeah.

MARILYN. Shrewd.

GINA.…so I'd be the, yeah. So I'd be the one sneaking off with fellas… (*To* ELAINE.) Remember Tony Gunshanin?

ELAINE. Jesus.

GINA (*to the others*).…or getting drunk, you know?

JANICE. Who was Tony Gunshanin?

ELAINE. Ah, this fella Gina went out with.

GINA. My first relationship.

HOLLY. Oh, really!

GINA. Or sexual one. If that's what you'd even call it.

MARILYN. What do you mean?

GINA. Ah, sure you know yourself: a fella that age, you may as well not even *be* there.

JANICE. Is that not a fella of *any* age?

They laugh.

Stuart's an exception, of course.

GINA. Ah no, *some* of them know what they're doing. (*Pause*.) You notice Holly's gone very quiet there!

HOLLY. Very funny.

JANICE. *And* Marilyn.

MARILYN. Huh? Fuck you!

ELAINE. Janice, see where they are now, will you?

GINA. I'm messing, Holly...

HOLLY. Right.

GINA.... I'm sure Maurice is a *very* accomplished lover.

MARILYN. What the hell?!

ELAINE. Don't give her any more drink.

GINA. Excuse me, I'm on the sparkling *water* now!

JANICE (*into phone*). Yeah, where are you? (*Beat*.) Oh right. (*To* ELAINE.) They're at the turn.

ELAINE. Great.

JANICE (*into phone*). All right. We'll see you now in a minute. (*Beat*.) All right, bye.

She ends the call.

ELAINE. Was he drunk?

JANICE. I couldn't say.

ELAINE. Could you guess?

JANICE. I'd guess they've had a few, yeah.

HOLLY. And what about *you*, Elaine?

ELAINE. What's that?

HOLLY. Would *you* be getting up to that kind of thing?

ELAINE. Fellas and whatnot?

JANICE. Ma was shy, isn't that right, Ma?

ELAINE. Not 'shy', I just wasn't that *in*terested.

GINA (*to* JANICE). Until your da came along.

ELAINE. That's right.

GINA. On his orange Vespa.

HOLLY. Did he have an orange Vespa?

MARILYN. Yeah.

GINA. Sure as soon as she got a look at *that*, she was gone – (*To* ELAINE.) weren't you?

ELAINE. Well, it wasn't just the *Vespa*, Gina.

STUART (*offstage; from outside*). All right, Felix?

JANICE. Here they are now.

MAURICE (*offstage*). You should have come *with* us, man. You'd have enjoyed it.

He enters, CIARAN *and* STUART *following.*

MARILYN. Well?

MAURICE. What?

STUART. Sorry, lads. Bursting. (*Hurrying upstairs.*) Some smell, Elaine!

ELAINE. Thanks, Stuart.

MAURICE. Yeah, remind you of Sundays, wouldn't it.

JANICE. Mm.

MARILYN. How was it?

MAURICE. Grand. Guess who we met…?

ELAINE. And how many'd you have?

MAURICE. Just a couple.

ELAINE. What's that? Three or four?

MAURICE. No, not three or four. Two or three.

MARILYN. Is that right, Ciaran?

CIARAN. Uuh…

MARILYN. Yeah, exactly!

CIARAN. No it is. I was just…

ELAINE. Sit down. Some of you'll have to eat off your laps.
There's your YR, Holly.

HOLLY. Oh. Thanks.

MAURICE. This is fantastic, Ma.

CIARAN. Absolutely.

ELAINE (*offering her a plate*). And this is yours, Gina. (*Then
switching it for another.*) No, *that* is. That's the one without
courgettes.

MARILYN (*mocking*). Ah, did you do one special for Maurice,
Mam?

ELAINE (*putting the first plate in front of* MAURICE). Shut up.

MARILYN (*same tone, to* MAURICE). Is that okay for you?

MAURICE. Yeah.

MARILYN (*same tone*). Nothing else that might offend your
palate, no?

CIARAN. You don't like courgettes?

MAURICE. It's the consistency. Same with aubergines.

CIARAN. Right.

ELAINE.…*And* roasted peppers.

GINA. Jesus, Maurice…!

JANICE. Ah leave him alone. Sure we all have our foibles
regarding food. Look at *me*…!

MAURICE. Exactly.

JANICE.…I mean, who doesn't like roast *potatoes*?!

CIARAN. You don't like roast *potatoes*?!

MAURICE. Janice doesn't like *chocolate*, Ciaran.

HOLLY. You're joking!

JANICE. I know…

HOLLY (*as a plate is put in front her*). Thanks, Elaine.

JANICE.…I'm a freak.

MARILYN. And, by the way, Ma, I'm not sure courgette qualifies as traditional.

ELAINE. What do you mean?

MARILYN. In terms of it being a traditional Irish meal.

MAURICE. That's true.

ELAINE. And what has that got to do with anything?

MARILYN/MAURICE. You said it was gonna be a traditional Irish *meal*.

ELAINE. So?

MAURICE. And Marilyn's saying courgette doesn't *qualify*.

ELAINE. Oh. You have yours, Ciaran…

CIARAN. Yeah.

ELAINE. And Janice?

JANICE. Yeah, no, I'm good.

ELAINE (*calling*). Felix? (*Pause.*) Felix!

HOLLY. I'll do it.

STUART (*who has just returned from upstairs; of one of the plates*). This one mine, Elaine?

ELAINE. Uh… yeah.

HOLLY (*at the door*). Dad, do you want to come in for some dinner?

ELAINE (*to everyone*). Now. We've white wine… Where's the red…?

MARILYN (*pouring herself some*). Here.

MAURICE. Can I have a drop of that, Marilyn?

MARILYN. Yeah, hang on.

ELAINE.…Anything anyone else might need?

GINA. I'm not sure I got... (*Picks up her fork.*) No. It's fine.

MAURICE. No, I think we're fine, Ma.

ELAINE (*to* FELIX, *who has just entered*). Just here, Felix. (*As he sits; to* MARILYN.) And why doesn't courgette qualify as traditional?

MARILYN. Well, *we* never had it when we were young.

ELAINE. Yes you did.

MAURICE/JANICE. We didn't.

ELAINE. Really?

GINA. I think I'm still a little bit traumatised from that crossing, you know that?

STUART. Yeah, my stomach's still lurching a bit.

ELAINE. That's all the Guinness inside it.

JANICE. Exactly.

STUART. I wasn't *drinking* Guinness.

ELAINE. Well, whatever.

MARILYN. Can I just, uh...

MAURICE. What?

MARILYN.... before we get started, can I propose a little toast to Ciaran's mam...?

ELAINE. Oh, of *course*!

CIARAN. Marilyn...

MARILYN. No, it's important, Ciaran.

ELAINE. Of *course* it is!

GINA. What's, uh...?

ELAINE. Sorry, Gina. Ciaran's mam's quite sick.

GINA (*to* CIARAN). Oh, really!

ELAINE (*to* CIARAN). Is it okay to...?

CIARAN. Of *course*.

GINA (*to* CIARAN). Like, *very*? Or…

CIARAN. Yeah, but listen: the last thing I wanna do is depress everybody…

MARILYN. Don't be silly.

CIARAN.…or have you all feeling sorry for me…

GINA. And what is it?

CIARAN. It's cancer.

GINA. What kind? Ah, *Ciaran*…

CIARAN. Yeah, *every* kind at this point. She's been fighting it for years, but, you know…

GINA. Right.

HOLLY. And how long does she have, Ciaran?

CIARAN. They're saying a couple of months…?

HOLLY. Oh, *no*!

MARILYN. Mm.

CIARAN.…maybe three? Yeah, we're getting into those final stages now.

MARILYN. *He's* been amazing – (*To* CIARAN.) haven't you.

CIARAN. Stop.

GINA. With what?

MARILYN. Just with helping out. (*To* CIARAN.) You *have*, though. (*To the others*.) Goes over to the house every lunchtime…

HOLLY. Right.

MARILYN.…every evening after work…

JANICE. So what about now?

CIARAN. My brother's there at the moment. (*To* HOLLY.) He lives in Cork, but he's up for the week to help my dad.

HOLLY. Give you a break.

MARILYN. Well, they kicked him out!

GINA. Oh, no!

CIARAN. Yeah, well that's how, you know, I'm able to *be* here.

HOLLY. I see.

ELAINE. And you know what? We're thrilled you are.

STUART. Exactly. (*Raising his glass.*) To your mam, Ciaran.

ELAINE (*raising her glass*). To your mam.

MAURICE (*raising his glass*). To *all* of your family, actually.

GINA. Exactly.

EVERYONE (*raising their glasses*). To your mam! / To all of your family.

They drink, start eating.

STUART. Delicious, Elaine.

JANICE. Absolutely.

ELAINE. Ah, thanks, guys.

HOLLY. *Really* gorgeous.

They continue to eat.

JANICE (*to* ELAINE). I told you Kelly was getting married, didn't I?

ELAINE. Mm!

MAURICE. To the Gard.

JANICE. Gerry, yeah.

ELAINE. And are you going?

MARILYN. That's in Crete or something, is it?

JANICE. Malta. (*To* ELAINE.) Yeah, no, we're not really sure yet…

HOLLY. Ah, I'd say it's lovely there.

GINA. It is.

ELAINE. Have you *been*? Oh, you went with *Dave*!

GINA. Exactly.

JANICE. And what was it like?

GINA.... The prick!

ELAINE. Ah, Gina...

STUART. Fucksake! (*His phone is ringing*.) Sorry, lads. (*Answering*.) Hello? (*Rising, leaving the table*.) Hey, how's it going? Yeah, no, we're good, how's it going with *you*? (*Beat*.) Okay... (*Beat*.) Oh, really...

He exits, right.

JANICE. And what was it like, Gina?

GINA. Yeah, it was fine. He liked it more than me because of all the ancient shit...

MAURICE. What do you mean?

GINA. Like all the temples and all, whereas the only thing *I* was interested in were the beaches.

HOLLY. And how were *they*?

GINA. Busy.

HOLLY. Okay.

GINA. Like, it isn't the biggest *place*, you know?

ELAINE. And is she excited, Janice?

MARILYN. Jesus, Maurice! (*To* HOLLY.) You see how much salt he's using?

HOLLY. Don't look at *me*.

MARILYN. You see that, Ma?

ELAINE. Ah, Maurice.

MAURICE. I'm on holidays!

JANICE. And the butter as well, look?

MAURICE. Fuck off, the lot of you, would you? Jesus!

Pause.

JANICE. The broccoli's lovely, Ma.

ELAINE. You like that, Janice?

JANICE. Mm.

ELAINE. Al dente.

FELIX. Crunchy.

ELAINE. Sorry, Felix?

FELIX. Crunchy.

CIARAN. It is.

MARILYN. Did I ever tell you what Jenny O'Mara does with broccoli…?

STUART (*returning*). Sorry, guys.

JANICE. Who was it?

STUART. Who do you think?

JANICE. And?

STUART. It's fine. (*Sitting down.*) The kids can be a bit tricky sometimes, Holly.

HOLLY. Right.

JANICE. Especially Tom. (*To* STUART.) *Was* it Tom?

ELAINE. Ah, he's a dote!

MAURICE. He is.

MARILYN. So is *she*, though.

GINA. Ah, they're *gorgeous*, lads.

STUART. They are. Just…

HOLLY. *So* adorable.

STUART. No, of course, but just, Mam and Dad sometimes find them a bit of a challenge.

JANICE. It's sorted, though, is it?

STUART. Yeah.

JANICE. Good.

   Beat.

CIARAN. The joys of parenting, huh?

STUART. Stop.

JANICE. Well, you can never really switch *off*, you see, is the…

CIARAN. Right.

JANICE.…the hardest thing, you know?

ELAINE. I've *been* there, Janice…

JANICE. I know.

ELAINE.…three times over.

GINA. Any sign of *you* surprising us any time soon, Marilyn?

MARILYN. Huh?

ELAINE. Sure Marilyn's still a child herself.

MARILYN. Very funny.

MAURICE. Thirty-two going on twelve.

JANICE (*to* MARILYN). I can't imagine you as a mother.

MARILYN. What?! That's a *horrible* thing to say.

JANICE. Ah no, I don't mean it like *that*.

MARILYN. You know what? I might have one someday now just to spite you all.

ELAINE. Ah, *that's* not a reason to do it.

MARILYN. I'm messing, Ma.

GINA (*to* MAURICE *and* HOLLY). What about you lads?

MAURICE. Hm? Oh, right.

HOLLY (*simultaneously*). Yeah, who knows? (*Long pause; then.*) What?

GINA. Nothing.

HOLLY. Why are you staring at me?

GINA. Your face is red.

HOLLY. It's *red*?!

ELAINE. Show? (*She does; beat.*) Ah, Holly…!

HOLLY. What?

ELAINE.…you're not *pregnant*, are you?

HOLLY. *No! God* no.

ELAINE (*to* MAURICE). *Is* she?

He doesn't answer.

MARILYN (*to* HOLLY). You're joking!

ELAINE (*to* HOLLY). How long?!

HOLLY (*to* MAURICE). You're an asshole, you know that?

MAURICE. *What…?!*

MARILYN. Ah, lads!

HOLLY (*to* ELAINE). Nearly fifteen weeks.

ELAINE. Oh, my *God*…!

MAURICE (*to* HOLLY).…What did *I* do?

MARILYN (*to* JANICE) Did *you* know?

JANICE. Yeah.

ELAINE.…I can't believe it!

GINA. Congratulations, Holly.

HOLLY. Thanks.

MAURICE. *And* Maurice.

GINA. And Maurice! Of course!

ELAINE (*to* HOLLY). And of course you're not *drinking*!

HOLLY. No.

ELAINE. Never even occurred to me.

MARILYN. Ah, I think we would have gotten suspicious eventually.

MAURICE. Well, we were hoping to make an announcement.

GINA. Shit. And I ruined it. Sorry, Maurice.

MAURICE. Don't be silly.

GINA. Sorry, Holly.

ELAINE (*goes to* HOLLY, *hugs her*). Congratulations, love.

HOLLY. Thanks, Elaine.

MAURICE (*as* MARILYN *does the same*). Ah for fucksake.
  So *everyone* has to go around the table hugging her now?

MARILYN. Shut up. Congratulations, Holly.

CIARAN. Congratulations, Holly.

STUART. Congratulations, Holly.

HOLLY. Thanks, guys.

GINA. Did *you* know, Felix?

FELIX. No.

GINA. And what do you think?

FELIX. Yeah, good. Very happy for her.

MARILYN (*to* JANICE). And how long did *you* know?

JANICE. Huh? I dunno, a week?

HOLLY. Yeah, about that.

MARILYN. Right. (*To* MAURICE.) Privileged information, is it?

MAURICE. No, she just…

HOLLY. I just wanted to talk to someone who had experience.

ELAINE. You could have talked to *me*, Holly.

HOLLY. No, but someone more my *age*, you know?

GINA. *Excuse me!*

ELAINE. *Exactly!* Bloody *cheek* of you!

HOLLY. No, but you know what I mean.

   Beat.

STUART. Big adventure.

HOLLY. Sorry?

STUART. Big adventure, like.

MAURICE. Right.

STUART. Your life's gonna change in ways you can't even imagine.

GINA. You know what? (*Raising her glass.*) To Holly and Maurice and the creation of new life.

EVERYONE (*doing the same*). To Holly and Maurice.

ELAINE. Congratulations, guys. Thrilled for you.

CIARAN. Absolutely.

ELAINE. Thrilled.

Everyone drinks; beat.

Ah, fuck it.

She goes to HOLLY *and hugs her again.*

MAURICE. Ah, Jesus.

ELAINE *hugs him too.*

Very good. Enough of the hugging now, all right?

Everyone laughs, says 'Awww', etc.

STUART. Actually, speaking of babies… guess who we met in Lynch's.

MAURICE. Oh, that's right…!

ELAINE. Who?

STUART. Aonghus!

ELAINE. Aonghus is *here*?!

MARILYN (*simultaneously*). You're joking!

JANICE. And what has Aonghus to do with babies?

MAURICE. He has one.

JANICE. He doesn't!

MAURICE. He's married and all now, yeah.

HOLLY. Who's Aonghus?

MAURICE. Marilyn's ex.

ELAINE. And *you* met him, Ciaran?

CIARAN. Yeah.

GINA. Was that awkward?

CIARAN. No, not really.

JANICE (*to* STUART). And is it a boy or a girl?

STUART. Couldn't tell you.

ELAINE. She's Irish, though, is she?

STUART. Who?

ELAINE. The wife.

STUART. Couldn't tell you that either.

ELAINE. Maurice?

No answer.

Did youse talk to the fella at *all*?!

GINA. Why wouldn't the wife be Irish?

MAURICE. Because he was living in Germany.

GINA. Ah.

JANICE. And what *else* can you tell us?

MAURICE. Um…

Beat.

JANICE. Jesus!

MAURICE.…he has a beard.

JANICE. 'He has a beard'…

STUART. That's right.

JANICE.…Bloody men! Have you no interest whatso*ever* in what's going on in each other's lives?

MAURICE. Ah, don't make it a gender thing.

JANICE. But you don't.

CIARAN. He wrote a book of poetry.

ELAINE. Really!

MAURICE. That's right. Had it published and everything.

ELAINE. Wow!

JANICE. The love of your life, huh, Marilyn?

MARILYN. Hardly.

JANICE. Oh, sorry, Ciaran.

ELAINE. The love of her life *thus far*.

JANICE. Exactly.

MAURICE. Well, the most *enduring*, though.

HOLLY (*to* MARILYN). How long were you together?

MARILYN. About four years…

HOLLY. Right.

MARILYN. …four and a half

ELAINE (*to* JANICE, *who is taking her plate to the sink*). You *finished*?!

JANICE. Uh-huh.

ELAINE. You hardly ate *any*!

JANICE. What are you talking about? I ate loads.

MAURICE. Nice fella.

JANICE. Kind of weird, though.

STUART (*to* CIARAN). Yeah, you're a way better catch, man.

MARILYN. He *wasn't* weird.

JANICE (*sitting back down*). What was he?

MARILYN. *I* dunno…

JANICE. Immature.

MARILYN. He wasn't imma*ture*.

JANICE. In *some* ways he was.

MARILYN. In *what* way…? Oh.

JANICE. He'd never slept with a woman before he went out with Marilyn, Holly.

HOLLY. Really!

MARILYN. Mm.

HOLLY. And how old was he then?

JANICE (*to* MARILYN). About thirty, was it?

HOLLY. *Thirty?!!*

JANICE. Yeah.

HOLLY. *Ugh! Creepy!*

MAURICE. What?!

HOLLY. No, just, who by that age hasn't had at least a *couple* of partners?

JANICE. Mm.

HOLLY. ...you know? Especially men.

MAURICE. Yeah, but '*creepy*'?!

HOLLY. Well, *odd*, let's say.

MAURICE. He grew up on an island.

JANICE. Yeah, but it's not as if he never left it, Maurice.

There is a knock on the door.

ELAINE. What the hell?

STUART. Will *I* get that?

ELAINE. Do you mind, Stuart?

STUART. No, not at all.

He rises, heads for the door.

MAURICE (*to* HOLLY *and* JANICE). *I* dunno. You're both a bit bloody judgemental, I'd say.

STUART (*opens the door*). Oh.

VOICE (*offstage*). Is this inconvenient?

STUART. I... Well...

ELAINE. Who is that, Aonghus?

AONGHUS (*offstage; calling*). Heya, Elaine.

ELAINE. Jesus, we were only *talking* about you! Come in!

He enters, carrying a plastic bag. She goes to him, hugs him.

How *are* you?!

AONGHUS. Ah, you're having your dinner!

ELAINE. Don't worry about it.

JANICE. Hey, Aonghus.

AONGHUS. Hey, Janice. How are things?

ELAINE. You don't know Holly, do you...?

AONGHUS (*to* HOLLY). No, how you doing?

ELAINE.... Maurice's girlfriend. And this is her father, Felix.

AONGHUS (*to* FELIX). Hi. (*To* ELAINE.) So, listen: I shouldn't be interrupting your...

ELAINE. Stop. Will you *have* some, actually?

AONGHUS. No.

ELAINE. Sit down. Are you sure?

AONGHUS. Yeah, no, I'll be having something later.

JANICE. I love your beard, Aonghus.

AONGHUS (*sitting down*). Sorry? Oh...

ELAINE. Yeah, very distinguished, Aonghus.

AONGHUS. I have it a couple of years now, actually.

MAURICE. Very rugged, man.

ELAINE. Will you have a beer, then?

AONGHUS. Eh... (*Beat.*) yeah, sure go on.

ELAINE. Good man. (*Heading to the fridge.*) And we hear you're married now.

AONGHUS. That's right.

ELAINE. With a baby?

AONGHUS. Chloe, yeah. She's nearly two.

JANICE. And is your wife *from* here, Aonghus? Or…

AONGHUS. No, she's German.

JANICE. Right.

ELAINE. We were wondering, actually.

She hands him a beer.

AONGHUS. Thanks. Yeah, no, I met her in Düsseldorf when I was working there.

ELAINE. And are you back now?

AONGHUS. Yeah.

ELAINE. For good, though.

AONGHUS. Well, for the foreseeable future.

ELAINE. And how does your wife… What's her name?

AONGHUS. Birgit.

ELAINE. Birgit.

AONGHUS. Yeah.

ELAINE. And how does she cope with life on the island?

AONGHUS. Yeah, well, she grew up in, like, a fairly rural part of Germany…

ELAINE. Right.

AONGHUS. …fairly isolated, so…

GINA. Not a huge adjustment.

AONGHUS. Exactly.

ELAINE. You remember Gina, Aonghus.

AONGHUS. Of course.

MAURICE. And so, can you *speak* German, Aonghus?

AONGHUS. Yeah, a bit.

MAURICE. Say something.

AONGHUS. Like what?

MAURICE. I dunno.

AONGHUS. Kann ich bitte einen Bier haben?

GINA. Very good!

JANICE. What does that mean?

AONGHUS. 'Can I have a beer, please?' I only really know enough to get by.

ELAINE. And you had a book published!

AONGHUS. Yeah, I actually brought a few copies over. (*Taking some out of the plastic bag.*) Just in case you might want to…

JANICE. Wow.

AONGHUS. …to, yeah, to read them or whatever.

He starts handing them out; STUART burps.

JANICE. Stuart!

STUART. Jesus. Sorry.

CIARAN (*looking at one*). Beautiful cover.

MAURICE. Mm.

ELAINE. This is some achievement, Aonghus.

AONGHUS. Yeah, no, I'm pretty proud of myself.

STUART (*flicking through*). 'A Sullied Radiance'. Nice.

GINA (*also flicking through*). 'The Simian'… what is it?

AONGHUS. 'Soothsayer.'

GINA. Right.

MAURICE. What's a soothsayer?

AONGHUS. Like, a fortune teller.

MAURICE. Ah.

ELAINE. And what's a simian?

MARILYN. Like, a monkey, Ma.

HOLLY. And how does a monkey tell fortunes?

AONGHUS. Well, you'll have to read the poem to find out.

JANICE (*handing her copy back*). Well done, Aonghus.

AONGHUS. No, you can have it.

JANICE. Oh!

AONGHUS. Yeah, no, they're gifts. Just…

STUART. He's famous.

AONGHUS. Huh? Well, hardly.

MAURICE. No, you are. *I've* never met a published author –
(*To* HOLLY.) have *you*?

STUART. Poet.

MAURICE. Well, whatever. So, you know…

GINA…. we're in the presence of greatness.

AONGHUS. Stop.

MAURICE. Exactly.

ELAINE. And so, why'd you come back from Germany?

AONGHUS. I just got homesick, really.

ELAINE. Right.

JANICE. And your wife was okay with that? *What's* her name
again?

MAURICE. Birgit.

JANICE. Birgit.

AONGHUS. Yeah, no, she was fine, she liked the idea of giving
Chloe the same kind of upbringing *she* had…

ELAINE. Right.

AONGHUS…. or *I* had.

JANICE. And is she gorgeous?

AONGHUS. Birgit?

JANICE. No…

AONGHUS. Oh, Chloe. Ah, yeah. So is Birgit, though. Ha-ha.

ELAINE. And how did you meet, Aonghus?

AONGHUS. Just in a bar.

ELAINE. Uh-huh.

AONGHUS. With friends.

ELAINE. Right.

AONGHUS. Mutual friends.

STUART. Some of these poems have very artsy titles, Aonghus.

AONGHUS. What do you mean?

STUART. 'An Oedipal Artefact'?

AONGHUS. *Is* that artsy?

STUART. I don't know.

AONGHUS. There's one called 'Fart'.

ELAINE. Sorry?

AONGHUS. 'Fart'.

MAURICE. And I see one here called 'Scooby Doo'.

STUART. Right.

MAURICE. That's not artsy either.

AONGHUS. Yeah, but it's actually not *about* Scooby Doo.

MAURICE. What's it about?

AONGHUS. The Catholic Church, childhood abuse, all that.

MAURICE. Oh!

AONGHUS. Yeah, no, it's a fairly serious piece, so the title's kind of ironic or whatever.

MAURICE. I see.

Silence.

AONGHUS (*to* ELAINE). So this is for *Sean*, Maurice was saying.

ELAINE. Sorry, Aonghus?

AONGHUS. You all being here.

ELAINE. Yeah, well, given how much he loved the place.

AONGHUS. Yeah, no I get you. (*Beat.*) I get you. And so, what'll you do?

ELAINE. What do you mean?

AONGHUS. Will you raise a few glasses to him?

ELAINE. Ah, yeah…

AONGHUS. Nice.

ELAINE.…tell a few *stories*…

AONGHUS. He was a lovely man.

ELAINE. He was.

AONGHUS. A very *generous* man, actually. *I* remem…

STUART (*looking up from the book*). Ah, very good.

GINA. What?

STUART. 'Fart'.

AONGHUS. Did you read it?

STUART. Very *clever*, actually. (*Puts the book down.*) Good job, man.

AONGHUS. Thanks. (*Long pause.*) Anyway… I'd better be getting back.

ELAINE. Oh, no!

JANICE. Are you sure?

AONGHUS. Yeah, it was only a flying visit, drop in the books or whatever. And Mam'll be wondering where I am.

ELAINE (*seeing him to the door*). Oh, you're in your mother's?!

AONGHUS. Yeah, for the moment. It actually works out really well, to be honest. She's mad about Chloe…

ELAINE. Is she?

AONGHUS. Yeah, and her and Birgit *really* get on, so…

ELAINE. Right. Well, say hello to her for me, will you?

AONGHUS. Ah, of course. And thanks for the beer.

MAURICE. Sure I'm sure we'll see you around the island over the next day or two.

ELAINE. True.

MAURICE. Down in Lynch's again or whatever.

JANICE. Good to see you, Aonghus.

AONGHUS. Yeah, you too. Bye, Marilyn.

MARILYN. Bye.

He exits. ELAINE *closes the door behind him.*

ELAINE. Now.

STUART. Something else, Elaine.

ELAINE. Sorry, Stuart?

STUART. The dinner.

ELAINE (*sitting down*). Ah, thanks. (*To everyone.*) There's more potatoes, by the way.

MAURICE. No, I'm stuffed, Ma.

GINA. Yeah, me too.

ELAINE. Felix? Ah, you don't have to do that, Ciaran!

CIARAN (*bringing his plate to the sink*). No, you're grand.

MAURICE. Big lick, you.

JANICE. Maurice…!

MAURICE. I'm messing!

ELAINE. Felix?

FELIX. Hm?

ELAINE. More potatoes?

FELIX. No, thanks. (*Getting up*.) I might just actually… (*Holds up his cigarettes*.)

ELAINE. Yeah, go ahead.

FELIX. Yummy, though.

ELAINE. Huh?

FELIX. The potatoes.

ELAINE. Oh, really?!

FELIX. *Very* fluffy inside.

He picks up his beer, exits outside.

GINA. They were.

HOLLY. Mm.

GINA. Marilyn.

MARILYN. What?

GINA. Weren't the potatoes very fluffy inside?

MARILYN. Did none of you see that?

ELAINE. What?

MARILYN. He didn't even look at me once.

STUART. Who didn't?

MARILYN. Who just left?

STUART. Felix?

MARILYN. No, *not* fucking Felix. Aonghus.

GINA. *Did* he not look at you?

ELAINE. Probably felt a bit awkward, did he? Given your history…

STUART. True.

ELAINE.…and Ciaran being here.

MARILYN. He *spoke* to Ciaran. And if he was awkward, why bother dropping in at all?

GINA. Ah, it was nice. Just, you know…

JANICE. Yeah.

GINA.…paying his respects.

MAURICE. What are we, the Mafia?

ELAINE (*to herself, troubled*). Hmm.

JANICE. What?

ELAINE. No, I just wonder if maybe we should have invited him *over* after.

JANICE. Over?!

ELAINE. Yeah, with his wife maybe, and…

JANICE. Why?

MAURICE. *Ah*, no.

ELAINE. Why not?

MAURICE. Cos we don't have that re*lation*ship with him any more. Isn't that right, Marilyn?

JANICE. Sure did we ever?

MARILYN. Huh?

JANICE. No, I'm just saying, it's not as if there was an ease, like, or a connection there the way there might have been with Stuart…

MAURICE. Exactly.

JANICE.…or Holly, you know?

MARILYN. What the hell are you *talking* about?

JANICE. I'm just saying we didn't *see* him as much.

MARILYN. You saw him enough! How dare you!

MAURICE (*getting some more roast potatoes*). Are you not pissed off at him, Marilyn?

MARILYN. Huh?

MAURICE. Are you not pissed off that he wouldn't look at you?

MARILYN. I am, but that doesn't mean you have to pretend he wasn't anything *to* me.

MAURICE. We're not.

MARILYN. *Or* to you. You're talking about him as if he was just some casual fucking acquaintance…

JANICE. We're not.

MARILYN.…but he was a major part of my *life*, Janice…

JANICE. I know.

MARILYN.…for nearly five *years*. And so *what* if he happened to live far away. Or if he wasn't as fucking charming as Stuart. And so what if I was only his *first*, by the way, and I take, I'm sorry, Holly, enormous exception to your saying that's creepy.

HOLLY (*beat*). I…

ELAINE. Marilyn.

MARILYN. What?!

ELAINE. I'm not quite sure what you're annoyed about here.

MARILYN. I just don't want him spoken about as if he was just some asshole. Even though he was an asshole just now not *talking* to me.

MAURICE. Right.

MARILYN. But if he's just some asshole *generally*, or some *freak*, then that means *I'm* an asshole and a freak as well for going *out* with him for so long, and I'm *not* an asshole…

ELAINE. Fair enough.

MARILYN. Or a freak. That's all. (*Pause; to* JANICE.) What?

JANICE. Nothing.

MARILYN. Typical Marilyn, is it?

JANICE. Well…

MARILYN. Of course it is. Well, I'm gonna say what I feel, and I'm sorry for jumping on you *specifically*, Holly...

HOLLY. Listen...

MARILYN.... but...

HOLLY. No, look: I shouldn't have said what I said. I don't even *think* that.

MARILYN. What?

HOLLY. That it's creepy.

MARILYN. Well, I'm sorry.

HOLLY. Okay.

ELAINE. All right, so...

HOLLY. Well, I'm sorry too.

MARILYN. Okay.

Pause. STUART *looks up from Aonghus's book.*

STUART. Should read that 'Fart'.

ELAINE. Huh?

STUART. Telling you. *Very* good.

ACT THREE

ELAINE *and* GINA *sit together. It is very late. The room has been tidied, the table cleared. Aonghus's books sit in a pile on the counter.*

GINA. And they *never* ask you?

ELAINE. Not 'never'...

GINA. Right.

ELAINE. ...I mean I've babysat up at the house if they're out for a drink or a meal or whatever; but if they're away overnight...

GINA. And would they do that often?

ELAINE. What?

GINA. Go away overnight.

ELAINE. Ah, yeah, now and again; but whenever they do, you see, it's always *them* they ask...

GINA. *His* parents.

ELAINE. Yeah... never me.

GINA. And would you not *say* it to them?

ELAINE. No.

GINA. Why not?

ELAINE. What if their answer is something I don't wanna hear?

GINA. Like what?

ELAINE. *I* dunno, 'We don't trust you'?

GINA. Why the hell wouldn't they *trust* you, though?

ELAINE. I know. *I* dunno. (*Beat.*) Anyway...

GINA. No, it's a weird one all right.

ELAINE. Mm. (*Pause.*) So, what are your plans?

GINA. What do you mean?

ELAINE. Are you gonna stay in London? Or…

GINA. Yeah, I don't know, to be honest. I still have friends there…

ELAINE. Of course.

GINA.…Theresa…

ELAINE. Right.

GINA.…Collette…

ELAINE. And what do *they* think?

GINA. About what happened?

ELAINE. Uh-huh.

GINA. Ah, they're *disgusted*, Elaine. Then there's my job…

ELAINE. But that isn't something you couldn't do from Dublin, is it?

GINA. No, I suppose.

ELAINE. Well, just to say that I'd *love* it if you came back.

GINA. Why?

ELAINE. So we could be in each other's lives again.

GINA. We *are* in each other's lives.

ELAINE. Ah, but *properly*, Gina…

GINA. Right.

ELAINE.…like we *used* to be. (*Beat; off* GINA*'s look.*) What?

GINA. When did you get so sentimental?

ELAINE. I'm not *being* sentimental. I'm being sincere.

GINA. I know.

STUART *enters from upstairs.*

STUART. You guys still up?

GINA. Hey, Stuart.

ELAINE. Yeah, just about.

GINA. How come *you're* down?

STUART. Can't bloody sleep.

ELAINE. Oh, no.

STUART (*getting a glass of water*). Ah, sure I'm always the same. New environment…

GINA. Right.

STUART.…or bed or whatever, I always have trouble dropping off. (*Takes a drink.*) We never celebrated *Sean*, Elaine.

ELAINE. Yeah, you know what…?

GINA. We were only saying.

ELAINE.…there was never a moment, really, that seemed appropriate.

STUART. Right.

GINA. And then, with Holly heading off early…

ELAINE. Exactly.

STUART (*nods; beat*). Do you reckon Marilyn pissed her off?

ELAINE. Ah no, sure were they not chatting away after?

STUART. I suppose. (*Beat.*) She's something else.

ELAINE. Marilyn?

STUART. Yeah.

ELAINE. Stop. Anyway, we'll have plenty of time tomorrow.

GINA. We will.

STUART. And have you *other* plans?

ELAINE. No, I think Maurice and *Holly* are gonna go for a swim.

STUART. Really!

GINA. You doing a fry?

ELAINE. Yeah, if any of us manage to get out of bed before midday. (*Looks at her watch.*) Jesus, speaking of which…

GINA. You off?

ELAINE. Yeah.

GINA (*as they rise*). All right. Gonna head myself in a minute. Night, sis.

ELAINE (*as they hug*). And I meant what I said, by the way. About...

GINA. I know.

ELAINE. All right. Night, Stuart.

STUART. Night, Elaine.

ELAINE *exits upstairs. Long pause.*

What did she say?

GINA. Huh?

STUART. That she meant.

GINA. Oh. She wants me to move back to Dublin.

STUART. Ah right. And are you gonna?

GINA. Yeah, I don't know. I'm not sure all this has even begun to sink *in* yet, to be honest.

STUART. Of course. (*Long pause.*) You all right?

GINA. How the hell did I not see it coming?!

STUART. Ah, Gina...

GINA. No, but there must be *some*thing I could have done.

STUART. There wasn't.

GINA. How do *you* know?

STUART. I *don't*, but you have to understand, men struggle with those kinds of questions far more often than you might *think*...

GINA. Come on.

STUART. ...those, yeah, those kind of existential...

GINA. *You* don't.

STUART. Well, I'm younger than Dave.

GINA. Okay.

STUART. And who *says* I don't? Listen: try adding *children* to the equation, you know? Not that mine aren't...

GINA. Right.

STUART. ...like, the best thing that's ever happened to me, but yeah. I mean, that's a big fucking *shock*...

GINA. Mm-hm.

STUART. ...like, a *big* fucking change, you know? Hey, Felix.

FELIX (*who has just entered from outside*). You haven't got a lighter, have you?

STUART. No, uh...

FELIX. Mine's stopped working.

GINA. There might be one in the drawer. Hang on. (*Goes to the drawer and looks.*) Ah. (*Finds a box of matches, brings it to him.*) Here you go.

FELIX. Thanks.

He exits again, closing the door behind him.

GINA. I forgot he was out there.

STUART. Mm.

GINA. You were saying...

STUART. I, uh...

GINA. The shock of having kids.

STUART. Oh, right. Yeah, well you saw your*self* how much attention they need.

GINA. You guys are amazing, though.

STUART. Well, we don't have much of a choice, really...

GINA. True.

STUART. ...you know? No, but we *do* make a fairly good team, I suppose. The worst thing *there*, though, is, you finally get to bed, where you can give each *other* a bit of attention, and it never happens…

GINA. Right.

STUART.… you end up just going to sleep.

GINA. Why, because you're exhausted?

STUART. Well…

GINA. What?

STUART. The woman is. And under, like I said, understandably so.

GINA. But *you're* not.

STUART. Huh?

GINA. The man isn't.

STUART. Well, the man *never* is, you know?

GINA. Hah. I do. (*Beat.*) Animals.

STUART. What?

GINA. You're animals. (*Beat.*) I don't know how any of you do it.

STUART. Men?

GINA. Women. Any of you. Parents.

STUART. Yeah, well, I look at someone like *you* and…

GINA. Someone like me?

STUART. Like, single…

GINA. Right.

STUART.… no responsibilities…

GINA. No partner.

STUART. Will that not be *good* for you in some ways, though?

GINA. In what ways?

STUART. *I* dunno. In the freedom it'll give you.

GINA. I'm still not sure that'll outweigh the *lone*liness, Stuart.

STUART. You won't be lonely for long.

GINA. Why not?

STUART. *Come* on.

GINA. Do you know how *old* I am?

STUART. Yeah, and you know what? The last time we saw each other was Sean's funeral, and I reckon you're more attractive now than you were back then.

GINA. Give me a break.

STUART. Seriously.

GINA. Well, that's nice of you, but you know what I mean?

STUART. About loneliness?

GINA. Yeah.

STUART. I do, but at least you have the, that's what I'm saying, the freedom to go and have that assuaged. I mean, however briefly.

GINA. Assuaged.

STUART. Like, sexually, whereas someone like *me*…

GINA. But you're not *lonely* sexually.

STUART. Well…

   Beat.

GINA. Okay.

STUART. …you know?

GINA. Well, that's between you and Janice.

STUART. Yeah, but Janice is kind of the *problem*, though.

GINA. I thought you said having *kids* was the problem.

STUART. You…

GINA. Look: either way, I'm starting to feel a little bit awkward talking about it. Do you mind?

STUART. No, of course.

GINA. I just…

STUART. Of course. No, that's fine.

Silence.

Oh, God…

GINA. What?

STUART.…You don't think I was being weird there with you, do you?

GINA. No, not at all.

STUART. Are you sure? I'm just going back in my head now and thinking, 'Jesus, *that* could be taken wrongly…'

GINA. Stuart…

STUART. '…*this* could be taken wrongly…'

GINA.…I don't think you were being weird at all.

STUART. Are you sure, now?

GINA. Yes.

STUART. All right. (*Beat.*) Well, look… (*Rises.*) I'll head back up before I start talking shite again. Actually, I think that's often all you need…

GINA. Hm?

STUART.…like, a chance to articulate, I suppose, your frustrations or whatever. So, uh… yeah. Thanks for listening, Gina.

GINA. No problem.

STUART. Night.

GINA. Night, Stuart.

He exits upstairs. Silence. She goes to the front door, opens it.

Are you not cold out there, Felix?

FELIX (*offstage*). Yeah, it *is* getting chilly, actually.

GINA. Do you want a jacket?

FELIX (*offstage*). Nah, that's okay.

GINA. All right.

She closes the door, pours another drink, sits down. Pause. It opens again and FELIX *enters.*

FELIX. Maybe I *will* get a jacket, actually.

GINA. Sure stay inside with *me*.

FELIX (*beat*). Uh…

GINA. Close the door if you are, though.

FELIX (*beat*). Right.

He goes to the door, closes it, returns, stops. Pause.

GINA. What is it?

FELIX. Wondering whether or not to have one for the road.

GINA. Right.

FELIX (*long pause*). Ah, sure… (*Beat.*) Fuck it.

He goes to the fridge, gets one, sits. Silence.

GINA. So quiet.

FELIX. Mm.

Silence.

GINA. So, what's *your* story?

FELIX. What do you mean?

GINA. Like, how come you're here?

FELIX. Oh. (*Beat.*) Well, Holly invited me.

GINA. Right.

FELIX. She was worried about my not getting out of the house enough…

GINA. And did you know everybody before?

FELIX. I knew Maurice…

GINA. Right.

FELIX. …but none of the others. (*Beat.*) They're nice.

GINA. Hm? Ah they are, yeah.

Long pause.

FELIX. I was sorry to hear about your break-up.

GINA. Oh.

FELIX. How long were you together?

GINA. Thirteen years? Yeah, unlucky for some. How long were you with your wife?

FELIX. Twenty-two.

GINA. Jesus.

FELIX. Mm.

GINA. And what happened?

FELIX. Same as yourself.

GINA. She *left* you?!

FELIX. Yeah.

GINA. Oh right. For some reason I thought she'd *died*! (*Beat.*) And why did she *leave* you?

FELIX. Fell in love with another fella.

GINA. Oh *no*!

FELIX. An Australian fella.

GINA. Oh that's *awful*, Felix!

FELIX. Yeah, that's where she's been living now the last ten years or so.

Long pause.

GINA. And are she and *Holly* close? Or…

FELIX. God, no. Holly *hates* her.

GINA. Right.

FELIX. Well, it wasn't just me she *left*, you know?

GINA. No, of course. (*Beat.*) Of course. (*Pause.*) But you've had relationships *since* then, have you?

FELIX. No.

GINA. Even *casual* ones, though.

He shakes his head.

Jesus… (*Beat.*) *I* couldn't do that.

FELIX. What?

GINA. Go for that long without being held by a man? Or being made feel like I was beautiful?

FELIX. Right.

Beat.

GINA. You're supposed to tell me I am.

FELIX. What?

GINA. Beautiful.

FELIX. Oh! Hah. Well, you are.

GINA. And was this, like, a conscious decision? I'm joking, by the way.

FELIX. No, no…

GINA. It wasn't.

FELIX. Well, *I* dunno. The opportunity just never presented itself.

GINA. Right. (*Pause.*) And what if it did?

FELIX. What?

GINA. Present itself.

FELIX. Well, it wouldn't.

GINA. But what if it did? (*Beat.*) Like, what if I said to you right now, come down to my room and ravage me…

FELIX. 'Ravage you'!

GINA. Yeah, or make love to me…

FELIX. That wouldn't happen, though.

GINA. Why not?

FELIX. Sure look at me.

GINA. Jesus, you've a very low opinion of yourself, Felix.
I mean, you're getting on a bit, and you're not in the best of
shape, but this 'look at me' shit, as if you're unattractive, is
nonsense, because you're not unattractive at all.

FELIX. Give me a break.

GINA. You're not.

Long pause.

FELIX. What?

GINA. So come on.

FELIX. You're joking.

GINA. No I'm not.

FELIX. 'Go to your room.'

GINA. Yeah.

FELIX. *Why*, though?

GINA. Why not? We're both unattached...

FELIX. Yeah, but...

GINA. ...we're both of a legal age...

FELIX. ...but what would the *purpose* be?

GINA. The pleasure.

FELIX. Right.

GINA. The company. *I* don't know, the human fucking...
connection, Felix.

Silence.

FELIX. Do you mind if we don't?

GINA. Oh.

FELIX. I just... it isn't something I'd ever feel comfortable
doing.

GINA. Okay. (*Beat.*) Can I ask why not?

FELIX. Because it isn't something I'd ever take lightly, or something I'd ever *do* lightly...

GINA. Right.

FELIX. ...without, you know, having gotten to know the other person really well, or having, even, feelings for the other person. And I know that sounds old-fashioned, or...

GINA. No, not at all.

FELIX. ...or prudish...

GINA. It doesn't. I admire your integrity, to be honest. (*Long pause*.) Anyway...

She rises, takes her glass to the sink, rinses it, then stands there, unmoving.

FELIX. Are you okay?

GINA. Uh-huh.

FELIX (*beat; then rising*). Ah, Gina...

GINA. It's fine.

FELIX. ...Don't cry.

GINA (*turning to face him*). It's fine, I just... I'm not in the most amazing place at the moment.

FELIX. I'm sure.

GINA. ...you know?

FELIX. Of course you're not. (*Beat*.) Here...

He goes to her, embraces her awkwardly.

GINA. Thank you, Felix.

FELIX. ...Maybe *this* is all you need.

GINA. Maybe.

Silence.

Felix...

FELIX. Sorry...

He tries to back away.

GINA (*holding on to him*). No, stay where you are. (*Beat.*) Stay where you are.

FELIX.... I just... your proximity...

GINA. Of course.

FELIX.... and the fact that we were discussing, uh...

GINA. Stay where you are.

FELIX. Christ.

GINA. It's fine. (*Beat.*) It's fine. (*Long pause.*) They have a life of their own sometimes, don't they.

FELIX. Very seldom, in my case.

GINA. Well, that sounds very much like a compliment.

He smiles; beat; she kisses him; beat.

Come on.

FELIX. What.

GINA. *You* know.

FELIX (*beat*). Gina...

GINA. Come *on*.

FELIX. I...

GINA. Ssshh.

She kisses him again, then takes his hand.

Come on.

She leads him off, left. Silence.

MAURICE (*offstage*). Holly.

HOLLY enters from upstairs, carrying a pillow and a duvet.

(*Offstage.*) Holly.

HOLLY. Just leave it.

MAURICE (*entering behind her*). So, what, you're just gonna *stay* down here?!

HOLLY. Uh-huh.

MAURICE. Just…

HOLLY. Better than sleeping with *you*.

MAURICE. Just because I don't wanna *talk* about it.

HOLLY. Well, you *don't* wanna talk about it.

MAURICE. No…

HOLLY. Exactly.

MAURICE.…not at, whatever, nearly three o'clock in the morning!

HOLLY. Fine. Off you go, so.

Silence.

MAURICE (*finally*). Go on, then.

HOLLY. What?

MAURICE. *How* did I undermine you?

HOLLY. You jumped on me in front of your whole fucking *family*, Maurice!

MAURICE. I…

HOLLY (*impersonating him*). 'Creepy?! Why are you calling him creepy?!'

MAURICE. Well, why *were* you?

HOLLY. I *told* you I meant to say 'odd'. I *told* you I used the wrong fucking word. And then you sit back while your *sister* attacks me?!

MAURICE. She didn't attack you…

HOLLY. Yeah, well, you *would* say that.

MAURICE.…she let you know you were out of line.

HOLLY. For offering up an opinion.

MAURICE. For offering up an *insensitive* one. And she apologised to you, didn't she.

HOLLY. Is that what you call an apology?

MAURICE. Christ.

HOLLY. Yeah, I'm so annoying, amen't I.

MAURICE. Holly…

HOLLY. So insensitive, as you put it.

MAURICE. I just don't understand why you can't admit when you've done something *wrong*…

HOLLY. Well, *I* can't…

MAURICE. …*Ever*. Or *said* something wrong.

HOLLY. Well, *I* can't understand why you always side with other people *against* me. Why do you do that, Maurice?

MAURICE. I don't.

HOLLY. Who is he to you anyway?

MAURICE. Who?

HOLLY. Whatever his name is.

MAURICE. Aonghus? Nothing.

HOLLY. So why are you siding with him against me?

MAURICE. I'm *not* si… *What?!*

HOLLY. You are.

MAURICE. I'm not siding with *any*body. I'm saying that, just because a fella's a late, whatever, bloomer, doesn't mean…

HOLLY. And then telling them all I was pregnant.

MAURICE. Jesus, I can't keep *up* with you. Who?

HOLLY. *You!*

MAURICE. They'd already *guessed* you were pregnant.

HOLLY. They hadn't guessed.

MAURICE. They knew from your… What the fuck are you *talking* about?

HOLLY. We said we'd announce it tomorrow night.

MAURICE. Yeah, but…

HOLLY. Fucking basking in the attention. Mammy's favourite. Everyone's favourite, and fuck how Holly might feel…

MAURICE. Ah, here, you know what…?

HOLLY.… Fuck Holly *altogether*. What?

MAURICE. I'm sick of this.

HOLLY. Of what?

MAURICE. Of *this*! Of having to, *constantly*, predict what is or isn't gonna upset you. Even your *father* has to be careful.

HOLLY. No, he doesn't.

MAURICE. Why is he here, then? You think he's enjoying himself?

HOLLY. Yes.

MAURICE. He doesn't *want* to be here.

HOLLY. So, why did he come, then?

MAURICE. Because he knew, if he didn't, the kind of shit he'd have to put *up* with from you. Same reason *I* always do what you want…

HOLLY.… that you always…

MAURICE. Yes. To avoid your… (*Beat; then, despairingly.*) And they all think you're such a sweet person. They all…

HOLLY. You fuck.

MAURICE.… They all worry about how *I* treat *you*.

HOLLY. They *should* worry.

MAURICE. Sorry?

HOLLY. Who's a fucking domestic abuser?

MAURICE. What?

HOLLY. Who's the physical...

MAURICE. Twice.

HOLLY.... the...

MAURICE. Twice that happened, and don't go on as if I punched your head in. I slapped you.

HOLLY. Hard.

MAURICE. And I threw you against the...

HOLLY. Hard. You saw what you did to my back.

MAURICE. And my guilt about that...

HOLLY. You're not guilty.

MAURICE. I am, and that guilt has allowed you to keep me under your thumb ever since, and I'm fucking sick of it. (*Beat.*) I'm sick of it. (*Beat.*) Christ, if you weren't fucking pregnant...

HOLLY. What. (*Pause.*) What.

MAURICE. Nothing.

HOLLY. You'd leave me?

MAURICE. I've signed my life away!

HOLLY. *Leave* me.

MAURICE. I can't!

HOLLY. What's stopping you?

MAURICE. I...

Beat.

HOLLY. You think I can't raise it on my own?

MAURICE. I'm afraid of *how* you might raise it. That baby is mine as well, and I have an obligation to it, and if that means staying with you, then so be it. Putting up with your selfishness and your anger and whatever else, then so be it...

HOLLY. How dare you?

MAURICE....I'll do it.

HOLLY. Why don't I just abort it?

MAURICE. What?!

HOLLY. Solve *all* your problems. That way, you won't be obliged to me any more and you can *have* your fucking freedom, if that's what you want so much. (*Long pause.*) Why aren't you answering?

MAURICE. That's your decision, Holly.

HOLLY. Well...

MAURICE. Not mine.

HOLLY. Well, you're not giving me many other options, are you?

Silence.

MAURICE. You know what? You go up.

HOLLY. Huh?

MAURICE. You go back to bed. I'll stay down here.

HOLLY. Oh, of course. Mister Moral-High-Ground.

MAURICE. What?

HOLLY. Mister Righteous. *You* get to be the one hard done by.

MAURICE. *I'll* go up, then. (*Long pause.*) What?

HOLLY. Fuck you.

She picks up the duvet and pillow, exits upstairs. MAURICE *sits down. Pause. He starts crying. A knock on the front door.*

MAURICE. What the fuck?

He stops crying, wipes his face. Another knock. He gets up, opens it.

Hey. (*Beat.*) What's up?

AONGHUS (*offstage*). Can I come in for a minute?

MAURICE. Everybody's in bed.

AONGHUS (*offstage*). Just for a minute.

MAURICE. Jesus. (*As he lets him in.*) Be quiet, all right?

AONGHUS. Have you been crying?

MAURICE. No!

AONGHUS. Are you sure?

MAURICE (*closes the door*). Aonghus, what do you want?

AONGHUS. I need to talk to Marilyn.

MAURICE. Marilyn's up in bed.

AONGHUS. I'll just be a minute.

MAURICE. Yeah, but she's up in bed. Can you not just do it tomorrow?

AONGHUS. No.

MAURICE. Why not?

AONGHUS. Cos I need to do it tonight, Maurice. (*Beat.*) Come on, I'll just be a minute. (*Pause.*) Maurice…

MAURICE. Right! Fucking… sit down or whatever!

He exits upstairs. AONGHUS *sits. Silence.* MARILYN *enters from upstairs.*

MARILYN. Aonghus…

AONGHUS (*rising again*). Hey.

MARILYN.… What the hell?

AONGHUS. I know.

MARILYN. What's happening? Have you been drinking?

AONGHUS. No.

MARILYN. Well, what are you doing here? It's like, Jesus…

AONGHUS. Yeah…

MARILYN.… it's twenty to three in the morning.

AONGHUS. I just… I know, there's just a couple of things I needed to say to you.

MARILYN (*beat*). What things?

AONGHUS. Well... (*Beat.*) Who's that, is that Maurice, there?

MAURICE (*sitting on the stairs just out of sight*). Yeah.

AONGHUS. Could you give us a minute?

MAURICE. Man...

He gets up, starts coming down.

AONGHUS (*to* MARILYN). Or we could go outside.

MARILYN. Are you joking?

AONGHUS. It's warm.

MARILYN. It *isn't* warm, it's *cold*.

MAURICE (*of the cigarettes and matches on the table*). Whose are these, Felix's?

MARILYN. Yeah, I think so.

He takes one.

What are you doing?

MAURICE. I don't want to go bed yet. And you guys need your privacy.

AONGHUS. Sorry, Maurice.

MARILYN. And why does that necessitate your having a cigarette?

MAURICE. *I* dunno. So I don't feel like an idiot standing outside.

MARILYN. In front of who?

MAURICE. Well...

AONGHUS. Maurice...

MAURICE. I'm going. Don't take all night, now, all right?

He exits, closing the door behind him. Pause.

MARILYN. So...?

AONGHUS. It was good to see everyone earlier...

MARILYN. Uh-huh.

AONGHUS....your mam and all...

MAURICE (*entering again*). Need a coat.

He grabs one, exits again, closing the door behind him. Long pause.

AONGHUS. So, I've thought about you a lot these last few years…

MARILYN. Okay…

AONGHUS. I'm not gonna *deny* it, Marilyn.

MARILYN. Fine!

AONGHUS. …but *tonight*… (*Beat.*) I mean, *nothing* could have prepared me for how I felt when I saw you.

MARILYN. You didn't even look at me.

AONGHUS. I couldn't.

MARILYN. Aonghus…

AONGHUS. It all came flooding back.

MARILYN. What did?

AONGHUS. All of it. You and me. Did it not come flooding back for *you*?

MARILYN. No.

AONGHUS. We should never have broken up.

MARILYN. It didn't *work* between us, Aonghus.

AONGHUS. It *some*times didn't work. It often did.

MARILYN. It *some*times did.

AONGHUS. Remember Galway…?

MARILYN. I need to go to bed, Aonghus.

AONGHUS. …in Jurys Hotel?

MARILYN. How drunk are you?

AONGHUS. I'm not drunk at all. Sure could I do this if I was drunk?

He stands on one leg, wobbles.

MARILYN. You wobbled.

AONGHUS. No I didn't. Look…

He stands on one leg, wobbles.

MARILYN. You wobbled again.

AONGHUS. I didn't wobble, I'm grand. And *sober* you'd wobble.

MARILYN. Huh?

AONGHUS. Even *sober* you'd wobble, so…

MARILYN. Well then, why would you even do it to demonstrate?

AONGHUS. Demonstrate what? Look…

MARILYN. Aonghus…

AONGHUS.…just let me say this…

MARILYN. I have a fella, Aonghus!

AONGHUS. Yeah, but fuck him.

MARILYN. 'Fuck him'?!

AONGHUS. I *know* you and him don't have what we had.

MARILYN. No you don't.

AONGHUS. I do.

MARILYN. And what about your family?!

AONGHUS. Fuck them too.

MARILYN. How the hell can you even…?! (*Beat.*) So, you'd just leave them.

AONGHUS. Yeah, well… if they existed…

MARILYN. Sorry?

AONGHUS. Nothing. Yes, I would.

MARILYN. They don't *exist*?!

He doesn't answer.

So, why did you say they existed?

AONGHUS. I was embarrassed.

MARILYN. By what?

AONGHUS. Not having moved on, all right? Being back here, same old Aonghus.

MARILYN. Jesus, Aonghus. (*Beat.*) So, what happened in Germany?

AONGHUS. Nothing. I didn't like it.

MARILYN. You...

AONGHUS. I was homesick.

MARILYN. So you came back.

AONGHUS. And I didn't... Yeah, and I didn't want you all thinking I hadn't moved on with my life, or moved forward in some way or other.

MARILYN. Uh-huh.

AONGHUS....in my life. Apart from my book, of course.

MARILYN. So you made up a wife...

AONGHUS. Uh-huh.

MARILYN....and a daughter! Christ, do you know how extreme that is?

AONGHUS. I do.

MARILYN. How demented?

AONGHUS. Remember all the things we got up to, Marilyn?

MARILYN. What things?

AONGHUS. In bed. How inventive we were.

MARILYN. Jesus...

AONGHUS. How perverse. Well, not perverse, but inventive. Remember Jurys?

MARILYN. Aonghus, we never stopped fighting.

AONGHUS. Which is...

MARILYN. How many times did we end it?

AONGHUS. Yeah, which is normal for people whose spirits are wild and inspired and...

MARILYN. Give me a break.

AONGHUS. ...and poetic. I'm serious, Marilyn. What about all those talks we used to have?

MARILYN. What talks?

AONGHUS. About writing, and art...

MARILYN. Oh, right.

AONGHUS. ...and the artist's calling. I mean, are you proud of me?

MARILYN. Huh?

AONGHUS. Are you proud of my literary achievement?

MARILYN. I'm *happy* for you, Aonghus.

AONGHUS. There's one I wrote... Hang on a sec...

He goes to the counter.

MARILYN. What are you doing?

AONGHUS (*grabbing one of the books*). There's one I wanna read to you.

MARILYN. Why?

AONGHUS. Cos you inspired it. (*Flicking through the book.*) Or being *without* you did.

MARILYN. I don't wanna hear it, Aonghus.

AONGHUS. Just a couple of verses. (*Still flicking.*) Just so you can see how much my work has evolved since...

MARILYN. Aonghus, I don't wanna *hear* it!

AONGHUS (*stops*). Why not?

MARILYN. Cos you shouldn't even *be* here! Now, *please*!

AONGHUS. All right...

MARILYN. I'm *sorry*!

AONGHUS. All right. No, you're right. I'll let you get back to bed. (*Beat*.) Will you do me a favour, though?

MARILYN. What.

AONGHUS. Will you, over the next day or two, have just a really deep look inside yourself, and really consider whether what you have with this other fella compares to the passion and abandon and fucking... spontaneity we had?

MARILYN. Okay.

AONGHUS. Will you *do* that?

MARILYN. *Yes!*

AONGHUS. Okay. And just so you know, and I don't wanna scare you with this, but if, having done that, you *still* don't wanna get back together, or at least, you know, give it a try, then... (*Beat*.) then, I'm not sure I wanna go on, Marilyn.

MARILYN. On with what?

AONGHUS. With life.

MARILYN. Ah, for fucksake, Aonghus.

AONGHUS. Listen: I *know* it's inappropriate...

MARILYN. Yes, it is!

AONGHUS. ...I *know* it's extreme, but it's also a very romantic *act*, am I right?

MARILYN. No it's not.

AONGHUS. It's a balls-out *gesture*, Marilyn.

MARILYN. It's an *aggressive* gesture. It's a *manipulative* gesture.

AONGHUS. Well...

CIARAN (*entering from upstairs*). All right, look...

MARILYN. Ciaran...

CIARAN. ...I can't hold back any more. Sorry, love.

MARILYN. Have you been listening?!

CIARAN. Yeah. (*To* AONGHUS.) You need to fuck off.

AONGHUS. We're talking.

CIARAN. Yeah, but you need to fuck *off*, man. It's after three in the morning, and what kind of a fucking fool would I be if I let you try to steal my girlfriend without doing something about it?

AONGHUS. You're not right for each other.

CIARAN. Who says?

AONGHUS. It's obvious.

CIARAN. How is it obvious?

AONGHUS. Marilyn…?

CIARAN. Go home, man.

AONGHUS. Marilyn…

MARILYN. What?

CIARAN. Go home.

AONGHUS. …I love you…

MARILYN. Jesus.

AONGHUS. …I always have, and this fella, I'm telling you…

MARILYN. What?

AONGHUS. …he isn't right for you.

MARILYN. But I love him, Aonghus.

AONGHUS. I don't think you do.

MARILYN. I do, Aonghus.

AONGHUS. No, I don't think you do, and I think…

CIARAN (*to* MARILYN, *on 'think'*). Do you not want him to *go*?!!

MARILYN. I do.

CIARAN. Well, *tell* him!!

MARILYN. I need you to go, Aonghus.

AONGHUS. But…

CIARAN. She needs you to *go*, you fuck!!!

ELAINE (*entering from upstairs*). What's going on?

AONGHUS. Nothing. I was just…

CIARAN. He's being a fuck! Sorry, Elaine.

ELAINE. Guys, I'm not too sure that this is the time to be…

GINA (*entering from left*). What's going on?

AONGHUS. I was trying to have a quiet chat with Marilyn, and this clown won't let us.

CIARAN. No I won't.

ELAINE. Why not?

CIARAN. Because he's trying to steal her. (*To* AONGHUS.) And *you're* the fucking clown.

JANICE (*entering from upstairs,* STUART *behind her*). What the hell's going on?

CIARAN. He's trying to steal fucking *Marilyn* from me.

ELAINE. Aonghus?

AONGHUS. Look…

ELAINE. Are you drunk?

AONGHUS. I'm a *little* bit drunk.

CIARAN. You're locked!

AONGHUS. I'm far from locked. Could I do this if I was locked?

He throws a kick at CIARAN.

CIARAN (*leaping back*). Get the fff…

STUART. Ah, here, now…

AONGHUS. Could I do *this*?

He throws another one.

CIARAN (*leaping back*). Jesus!

STUART. Ah, listen, now. Enough of the, uh…

MARILYN. He needs to leave.

STUART. That's right. (*To* AONGHUS.) Listen, you need to *leave*, man.

MAURICE (*entering from outside*). What's going on?

AONGHUS (*ignoring him*). Marilyn...

STUART (*reaching for* AONGHUS). Did you not bloody hear what I...?

AONGHUS. Get your fucking...

ELAINE. Aonghus...

AONGHUS. Get your hands off me!

STUART. Out!

He grabs AONGHUS *and they struggle.*

JANICE. Stuart! Oh, God!

CIARAN moves in to give a hand.

AONGHUS. Get the fuck! Get the fuck! Marilyn! (*Beat.*) Marilyn, you're a dope!

STUART (*to* CIARAN). Grab his other arm!

AONGHUS. Do you not understand? I love you!

STUART. His arm!

CIARAN. I'm trying!

AONGHUS (*to* STUART). I told you to get your...

He lashes out, hitting STUART *in the face.*

JANICE. Stuart!

STUART. Agh, *fuck me!*

His nose is bloodied.

JANICE. Stuart!

STUART. I *heard* you, fucksake!

MARILYN. Maurice, help them, will you?

MAURICE *does. The three men wrestle* AONGHUS *toward the front door.*

They manage to throw AONGHUS *out, closing the door behind him. He bangs on it.*

AONGHUS (*offstage*). *Ass*holes!

MARILYN. Go home, Aonghus.

AONGHUS (*offstage*). Fucking *shit*heads! Open it!

MARILYN. Aonghus...

AONGHUS (*offstage*). Open the door, you fucking pack of... (*Bursts into tears.*) fucking *shit*arses!

He sobs a while, then goes silent. After several moments:

GINA. Is he gone?

MAURICE. Ssshh! Or not 'ssshh', just...

They continue to listen. Finally:

AONGHUS (*offstage*). Fuck it. (*Pause; then, from a little further away.*) Fuck youse all! Fucking dipshits. (*Beat.*) You can fuck off back to Dublin! (*Pause; then, even further away.*) After ripping my fucking top and everything...

They continue to listen. Finally, relaxing:

MAURICE. Jesus.

ELAINE. Mm.

STUART. We all okay?

JANICE. Are *you*?

STUART. Yeah, I'm grand.

JANICE. Are you sure?

STUART. Yeah, I'm *fine*, don't *worry* about it!

GINA. He has it bad for *you*, Marilyn.

MAURICE. Yeah, what the fuck? (*To* ELAINE.) You all right, Ma?

ELAINE. Yeah, no, my heart just…

JANICE (*to* MARILYN). So, he's happy to just walk out on his wife and daughter for you?!

CIARAN. They don't exist.

JANICE. They *what*?!

ELAINE. They don't *exist*?!

CIARAN. No, he made them up.

JANICE. Ah, here…

MAURICE. You're joking!

JANICE.…I always knew there was something wrong with that fella, but Jesus…

MARILYN. Don't start, Janice.

JANICE. *You* don't start. You see what he did to *Stuart*?!

STUART. I'm *fine*, what the…?

JANICE. Fucking *psycho*!

ELAINE. Janice…

JANICE. He *is*, though.

GINA. Well, we're all okay now, which is the…

JANICE (*to* MARILYN). Why do you always have to go for the crazy ones?

MARILYN. Don't start making this *my* fault, Janice.

JANICE. Why, though?

MARILYN. I don't.

JANICE. Him? Darryl Egan? You *do*.

MARILYN. Well, why do *you* always go for the fucking *shallow* ones?

STUART. Shallow?!

MARILYN. The narcissists.

STUART. *I'm* not a narcissist.

MARILYN. Fine.

STUART (*to* JANICE).... Am I?

JANICE. No.

MARILYN (*to* STUART). Well, you're certainly full of yourself.

ELAINE. Marilyn...

MARILYN. And entitled.

ELAINE.... Stop.

MARILYN. And self-important. I suppose, you know, like goes after like.

JANICE. Like you and your crazy boyfriends.

MARILYN. I'm not crazy.

JANICE. Well... there's some might disagree with that, Marilyn.

MARILYN. Like who?

GINA (*to* ELAINE). You know what it is? It's adrenalin.

MAURICE. Will I put on some tea?

CIARAN. I'm fine.

MAURICE. Tea, Ma?

ELAINE. No, you know what I think we should do...?

MARILYN (*to* JANICE). How am I fucking crazy?!

MAURICE. Marilyn.

MARILYN. What?

MAURICE. Leave it.

MARILYN. Miss Fucking Eating Disorder.

JANICE. Excuse me?

ELAINE. Maurice, check he's actually gone, will you?

MAURICE. Of course he's gone.

ELAINE. Check, though.

MAURICE. Jesus…

He heads for the door.

JANICE (*to* MARILYN). *What* fucking eating disorder?

ELAINE. Janice…

GINA. Lads, it's late. Will we not just…?

MAURICE opens the door and AONGHUS bursts in.

Oh, my God!

STUART. Grab him!

MAURICE. Ah, here, now.

AONGHUS (*as* STUART, MAURICE *and* CIARAN *do*). There's no need to grab me.

STUART. Hold him!

CIARAN. I am!

MAURICE. Ah, come on, now.

AONGHUS. There's no need to hold me, I only came in… I'm going, all right?

They release him; beat.

I only came in to say that you killed me, Marilyn. I can't live without you, *literally*, so you've killed me, all right?

ELAINE. What does that mean, Aonghus?

AONGHUS. You know what it means. (*To* MARILYN.) You've killed me. All right. I'm going. All right.

ELAINE. Aonghus…

AONGHUS. I'm going.

He goes. MAURICE closes the door behind him. Pause.

GINA. So, is he saying he's going to kill himself?

CIARAN. Yeah, kind of sounds like that.

ELAINE (*to* MARILYN). Do you think he's serious?

MARILYN (*quietly*). *I* dunno.

ELAINE. Marilyn…

MARILYN (*louder*). I don't *know*.

JANICE (*to* MARILYN). What fucking eating disorder?

MARILYN. Huh?

MAURICE. Ah, come *on*, for fucksake!

MARILYN. The one you suffer from, Janice.

JANICE. But I don't.

MARILYN. All right…

JANICE. And…

MARILYN.…*you* keep deluding yourself about that.

JANICE. You're so full of shit, you know that?

MARILYN. Fine.

JANICE. And if you think attacking me this way isn't gonna have consequences…

MARILYN. Hang on…

JANICE.…then…

MARILYN.…*you* attacked *me*.

JANICE. Huh?

MARILYN. You attacked me, saying every man I've been out with was fucking crazy!

JANICE. Well…

MARILYN. Saying *Ciaran's* crazy, how *dare* you!

JANICE. I didn't say *he* was crazy.

MARILYN. Well…

JANICE. Although the jury's still fucking out, to be honest.

MARILYN. Oh, very good. (*Beat.*) Very good. Well, whatever he is, at least he isn't unfaithful.

JANICE. Huh?

MARILYN. At least he isn't unfaithful.

JANICE. Meaning what?

MARILYN. Well, unlike some other people.

JANICE. Like who?

MARILYN (*beat*). Who do you think?

JANICE. Stuart? (*Beat.*) What are you talking about?

MARILYN. He tried to get me to give him a handjob at Deirdre Conway's wedding.

STUART. What the fuck?!

ELAINE. Marilyn, stop it.

STUART. What are you talking about?

JANICE. How could you say such a thing?

MARILYN. Cos it happened. Sorry, Stuart.

STUART. For what?

MARILYN. For telling on you.

STUART. It *never* happened!

MARILYN (*to* JANICE). I went up to get a cardigan out of my room…

STUART. This is…

MARILYN (*to* STUART) What? (*To* JANICE.) …and *he* walks in…

STUART. This is pure fucking invention!

MARILYN. …and says to me, 'Any chance of a wank, Marilyn?'

GINA. What?!

MAURICE. Ah, Jesus…!

MARILYN. Hang on a sec. So *I* say…

STUART (*to* MARILYN). You're a little fucking *cunt*, you know that?

ELAINE (*beat*). What the…

GINA. Jesus Christ!

CIARAN. *What* did you call her?

STUART. It didn't happen!

CIARAN. *What* did you call her?

STUART. What are you gonna *do* about what I called her?

CIARAN. I'll break your fucking face, Stuart!

JANICE (*beat*). You know what? We're out of here tomorrow. First fucking ferry!

MARILYN. Why don't you just go *now*?

JANICE. Where the fuck will we *go*?

MARILYN. I don't care. Go and sleep in a ditch or something.

JANICE. We're gone, do you hear me, Mam? As long as she's here, I'm not staying.

ELAINE. This is… I…

JANICE. Do you hear me, Mam! She's a fucking monster!

MARILYN. Fuck you.

STUART. You know something, Marilyn…?

JANICE. Don't even engage with the fucking bitch. Come on.

STUART (*as he and* JANICE *start upstairs*). I'm sorry, Elaine.

JANICE (*to* MARILYN). You're a fucking bitch!

MARILYN. Whatever.

STUART (*stops, turns; beat; to* MARILYN). I'm honestly baffled as to why you'd make up something like that…

MARILYN. Stuart…

STUART.…I really am.

He and JANICE *exit upstairs. After a moment:*

ELAINE (*to* MARILYN). Why would you do that?

MARILYN. Huh?

ELAINE. Why would you *say* that?

MARILYN. *She* was saying shit.

GINA. So it isn't true?

MARILYN. It *is* bloody true, and I wouldn't have opened my mouth if she hadn't *pushed* me the way she did. (*Off* ELAINE's *look*.) What?

ELAINE. You're amazing.

MARILYN. What do you mean?

ELAINE. Your selfishness.

MARILYN. Oh, fuck off.

ELAINE. Your destructiveness.

MARILYN. Well, maybe you should have a think about *why* I'm that way, Ma.

ELAINE. What are you talking about?

MARILYN. Nothing.

ELAINE. You know what, Marilyn...?

CIARAN's *phone rings.*

CIARAN (*answering*). Hello? Yeah, no, I'm up, what's happening? (*Pause.*) You're joking. (*Pause.*) But... (*Long pause.*) She's *okay*, though, is she? (*Beat.*) Well, either she is or she isn't, Rob. (*Pause.*) Ah, fuck! (*Beat.*) Ah, Jesus, and how is she *now*? (*Beat.*) Yeah, but how is she *now*, Rob?! (*Beat.*) Rob! (*Beat.*) Fucking *answer* me, will you!!!

ACT FOUR

The next morning. ELAINE *tidies.* FELIX *hums while eating cereal. A pot of coffee sits on the table.*

ELAINE. *You* seem very happy this morning, Felix.

FELIX. Do I?

ELAINE. Yeah.

FELIX. I don't know. I like the old Cheerios.

ELAINE. Right.

FELIX. *And* being here.

ELAINE. It's lovely, isn't it.

FELIX. Mm.

She continues to tidy. MAURICE *enters from right.*

MAURICE. So, what is it? Lucozade…

ELAINE. Yeah, paracetamol…

MAURICE. Right.

ELAINE.…and cotton buds.

MAURICE. That's it?

ELAINE. That's it. Oh, and the milk! Thanks, love.

MAURICE *exits outside.* JANICE *enters from upstairs.*

JANICE. Do you mind if I take some of that coffee?

ELAINE. Of course not.

JANICE *gets two cups from the press, starts filling them.*

So you're staying.

JANICE. Well, if *she's* going back…

ELAINE. All right, good.

JANICE. But it's over, Ma, and I know it's gonna make things hard for you in the future, but that's…

ELAINE. Okay.

JANICE.…I never want to be in the same bloody *room* as her again.

She takes her coffees and heads for the stairs.

ELAINE. Where are you going?

JANICE. They're here till twelve.

ELAINE. So?

JANICE. So what have I just been *saying* to you?

ELAINE. Oh right.

JANICE (*to* STUART *who has just appeared on the stairs*). I have them.

STUART. No, I just…

JANICE. What?

STUART. She's saying they're losing their minds.

JANICE. Ah, Stuart!

ELAINE. Who?

STUART. My mam and dad. They'd a tricky time with Tom last night, and she's saying they can't do another one, Janice.

JANICE. So, what then? I'm not going back.

STUART. Well, *one* of us has to.

JANICE. Jesus, why the hell does she offer to do these things and never follow through?

STUART. It's not *her* fault they're such hard work.

JANICE (*as if to his mother*). Yeah, well, don't agree, then…

STUART. I know.

JANICE.…we'll make some *other* arrangement.

FELIX (*rising, cigarettes in hand*). Sorry, guys…

ELAINE. Hm?

FELIX (*gesturing outside*)....just gonna...

ELAINE. Yeah, yeah.

STUART (*to* JANICE, *as he exits*). I have to go back.

JANICE. Okay.

STUART. Are you coming?

JANICE. I'm on my holidays, Stuart.

STUART. Okay. (*Beat.*) I'm sorry, Elaine.

ELAINE. Look, if you have to *go*, then...

STUART. *And* about last night, and I've said it already, I know, but I never did what she said I did. I know she's your daughter and all...

ELAINE. I know.

STUART. And I'm sorry I called her the c-word as well. Or that I used it in your presence, but I'd never heard anything, been *accused* of anything so, you know...

ELAINE. I know.

STUART. ....outrageous, like. All right. (*To* JANICE.) Gonna head back up.

JANICE. Yeah, I'm coming up *with* you.

ELAINE. So, are you *gonna* stay, Janice?

JANICE. Yeah. Or we'll see.

ELAINE. Ah, stay. It won't be the same without you.

JANICE. We'll *see*, Ma.

> *She and* STUART *exit upstairs.* ELAINE *takes Felix's cereal bowl to the sink, rinses it, starts making more coffee.* GINA *comes down the stairs, hair wet.*

GINA. Hey.

ELAINE. Hey.

GINA. Feel a bit more *alive* now, I must say…

She stops, noticing that ELAINE *is upset.*

Ah, Elaine!

ELAINE. I'm okay.

GINA. Ah, love!

She embraces her.

ELAINE. All I wanted was for us all to have a nice *time* together!

GINA. I know.

ELAINE. And not for *me*…

GINA. I know.

ELAINE.…for *Sean*. We never even *reminisced* about him.

GINA. So we'll reminisce about him later. I mean, fine, so you won't have Marilyn…

ELAINE. No, it looks like Janice is going too.

GINA. *Janice* is going?!

ELAINE. Stuart's mother says they can't handle the kids another night.

GINA. You're joking!

ELAINE. Fucking eejit. I'll tell you something: you wouldn't have *me* calling, begging them to come home and take them off *my* bloody hands…

GINA. Well, listen…

ELAINE.…*however* tricky they got.

GINA. Well, look: we can still…

ELAINE. Ah no, it won't be as *good*, Gina.

GINA. I *know* it won't be as good. It can still be *good*, though, no? *I'm* here…

ELAINE. I know, but…

GINA.....*Maurice* is here... Do you not think Holly and Felix'd be interested in hearing all the stories?

ELAINE. Mm.

GINA. It doesn't have to be a *complete* disaster.

MARILYN (*appearing on the stairs*). Is *she* in there?

ELAINE. No, she's up in her room. You know *they* might be leaving *too*?

MARILYN (*coming down, followed by* CIARAN). Today?

ELAINE. Yeah.

MARILYN. Why? His ma and da?

ELAINE. Mm-hm.

MARILYN. Sure I could've *predicted* that. Well, they'd better not be planning to go on the same bloody *boat* as we are.

GINA. How are you, Ciaran?

CIARAN. Agh.

GINA. C'mere.

She hugs him.

MARILYN (*to* ELAINE). No fry?

ELAINE (*gives her a look; then*). There's cereal there...

MARILYN. And what about coffee?

ELAINE. Do you not see me *making* another pot?!

GINA (*to* CIARAN). Did you sleep at all?

MARILYN. He sat up the whole night writing.

GINA (*to* CIARAN). Really?! What were you writing?

CIARAN. Her eulogy?

GINA. Ah!

MARILYN. It's beautiful.

CIARAN. Stop.

MARILYN. It is, though.

GINA (*to* CIARAN). Were you inspired by the *other* fella?

CIARAN. Who? Oh, *Aonghus*?!

GINA. Yeah.

CIARAN. Well, it isn't *poetry*…

GINA. Right.

MARILYN. It *is* poetry. (*To* GINA.) *I* think it's poetry.

CIARAN (*to* GINA). No, I was just compelled to put into words what she meant to me, you know…?

MARILYN (*to* CIARAN). Sure read it to them.

CIARAN. Huh? Ah, no.

GINA. Oh, I'd *love* to hear it, Ciaran. Elaine?

ELAINE. Uh-huh.

MARILYN. We *all* would, Ciaran.

CIARAN (*beat*). All right. (*Takes a folded up page from his back pocket*.) Kind of embarrassing. (*Unfolds it*.) So… (*Clears his throat, reads*.) 'Maura…' (*To* GINA.) Her name was Maura.

GINA. Okay.

CIARAN. So…

JANICE (*appearing on the stairs*). Mam…?

MARILYN (*to* JANICE). What boat are you getting?

JANICE (*ignoring her, continuing to* ELAINE).…have we any paracetamol?

ELAINE. Maurice is getting some.

MARILYN. Janice…

JANICE (*to* MARILYN). The twelve.

MARILYN. *We're* getting the twelve.

JANICE. I don't give a shit.

MARILYN. Get the four.

ELAINE (*to* JANICE). So you're going *with* him?

JANICE. Sorry, Ma. I have to. (*To* MARILYN.) Fucking cow,
    you.

MARILYN. *You're* a fucking cow!

    JANICE *exits upstairs again.*

GINA. Go on, Ciaran.

CIARAN. All right.

    He clears his throat.

MARILYN (*to* ELAINE, *who is staring at her*). What?

ELAINE. Nothing.

MARILYN. This isn't *my* doing, Ma.

ELAINE. Okay.

MARILYN. It isn't. *I* didn't ask him to come and declare his,
    whatever, undying love for me.

ELAINE. That's not what did the damage, Marilyn.

MARILYN. What is?

ELAINE. You know what is. Your story.

MARILYN. It wasn't a *story*.

ELAINE. Marilyn...

MARILYN. *No* now. Just because something's hard to *accept*,
    doesn't mean...

FELIX (*offstage; from outside*). All right, Maurice?

MAURICE (*offstage*). Felix.

FELIX (*offstage*). Looks like a beautiful one.

MAURICE (*calling back as he enters*). Yeah, we'll see.

MARILYN (*continuing to* ELAINE)….doesn't mean it didn't *happen…*

MAURICE. Doesn't mean *what* didn't…? Oh.

ELAINE. What did you get?

MAURICE. I got what you *asked* me to get… (*Taking each item out of a plastic bag.*) Milk…

ELAINE. Uh-huh.

MAURICE.…Lucozade…

ELAINE. Excellent.

MAURICE.…and cotton buds.

MARILYN. Did you get paracetamol?!

MAURICE (*looks at her; beat*). Oh, fuck.

ELAINE. Ah, for God's sake, Maurice…!

MAURICE. Of course I did. (*Producing them.*) Got a couple of packets.

ELAINE *takes one of them off him.* HOLLY *enters from upstairs, phone and charger in hand.*

HOLLY. Hey, lads.

ELAINE. Hey, Holly. How did you sleep?

HOLLY. Well, very deeply, *ob*viously. I heard about your mam, Ciaran.

CIARAN. Right.

HOLLY. You poor thing. How are you?

CIARAN. Yeah, you know…

HOLLY. Of course.

She plugs in her phone at the counter.

ELAINE. There's coffee there, Holly.

HOLLY. All right. Thanks, Elaine.

JANICE (*appearing on the stairs*). Did you get paracetamol, Maurice?

MAURICE. Yeah.

He holds up the second box.

JANICE. Throw it to me, will you?

MAURICE. Come down and get it.

MARILYN. She doesn't *wanna* come down.

JANICE. That's right.

MARILYN. She's making a point.

JANICE. I'm not making *any* point. I'm just fucking repulsed by *you*.

MARILYN. Look to your husband.

JANICE. Fucking deceitful...

ELAINE. All right...

JANICE....lying fucking...

MARILYN. Look to your husband, Janice.

JANICE (*mimicking her*). 'Look to your husband, Janice'! (*To* MAURICE.) Just throw it, will you?

He does; she fails to catch it.

MAURICE. Exactly.

JANICE (*coming down and picking it up*). 'Exactly'! If you'd done it *properly*...

FELIX (*entering from outside*). Sorry, uh... Elaine? There's someone down at the gate.

ELAINE. Who?

FELIX. Some woman.

MARILYN (*looking out the window*). Bernadette.

ELAINE. Bernadette? (*She exits outside; offstage; calling.*) Heya, Bernadette. (*Pause.*) Huh? (*Pause.*) Hang on, I'll come down to you.

JANICE (*to* MARILYN)....Fucking *wagon*, you!!

She exits back upstairs. MARILYN *pours herself some coffee.*

FELIX. Some day out there.

MAURICE. Mm.

FELIX. Nice day for a wander.

MARILYN (*holding up coffee pot*). Ciaran?

CIARAN. No, I'm okay.

FELIX. Anyone fancy a wander after?

GINA (*beat*). I'll have a wander with you.

FELIX. Really?

GINA. Yeah, sure why not?

MARILYN. Go on, Ciaran.

CIARAN. What? Oh...

MARILYN. Read it.

GINA. Oh yeah, go on. Ciaran stayed up all night writing a eulogy for his mam, Felix...

FELIX. Oh, really!

CIARAN (*unfolding his sheet of page again*). All right...

FELIX. *Very good!*

CIARAN....so, uh... yeah. Her name was Maura.

HOLLY. Okay.

CIARAN. All right. (*Clears his throat, then reads.*) 'Maura...'

GINA*'s phone rings.*

GINA. Shit. Sorry, guys. (*Checks it.*) Fucksake, sorry, Ciaran. (*She exits left while answering.*) Hello...?

MARILYN. Go on, Ciaran.

JANICE *enters from upstairs again. Everyone watches as she goes to the sink, fills a glass of water, returns to the stairs, stops, turns.*

JANICE. Why are you all so quiet?

MAURICE. Ciaran's about to read the eulogy he wrote for his mam.

JANICE. Ah, right.

She turns back to head up the stairs.

MAURICE. You're not gonna *listen*?!

JANICE (*stopping*). What? (*Then.*) Sorry, Ciaran. Go on.

CIARAN. You don't *have* to.

JANICE. No, go on, I'd *love* to hear it.

MAURICE. No pressure, Ciaran.

CIARAN. Yeah.

MARILYN. It's beautiful, Maurice.

MAURICE. I'm sure it is.

MARILYN. Like, really good.

MAURICE. Well, let us *hear* it, for fucksake!

MARILYN. Sorry. (*To* CIARAN.) Go on.

MAURICE. Sorry, Ciaran.

CIARAN. You're grand.

MAURICE. Go on, man.

CIARAN (*beat; reads*). 'Maura…' Ah, *fuck*sake!

ELAINE (*simultaneously, as she enters from outside*). Aonghus didn't… (*Then, to* CIARAN.) Sorry?

CIARAN. Sorry? Nothing.

ELAINE (*to all*). Aonghus didn't come home last night. *Go* home.

JANICE. So?

ELAINE. So everyone's getting worried. Where's Gina?

MAURICE. She, uh…

ELAINE. His mother thought he was still in bed, but then when she went to his room...

MARILYN. He's fine.

ELAINE. Says who?

MARILYN. Well...

ELAINE. How do you know? Do you not remember the things he was saying?

MARILYN. Ah, I wouldn't be minding *that*, Ma, *Jesus*...

ELAINE. You wouldn't be *minding* it?!

JANICE. Aonghus turned up at all hours this morning, Holly, and...

HOLLY. No, so I heard. I can't believe I slept through it.

ELAINE (*on 'slept through it'*). We need to help them look for him.

JANICE (*checking her watch*). Ma, we've to *go* in, like...

MARILYN (*to* ELAINE). All he's, listen, all he's doing is looking for bloody attention.

ELAINE. How do you know?

MARILYN. Cos I *know* him.

ELAINE. Yeah, but...

MARILYN. So do *you*, sure.

ELAINE. Yeah, but what if he's not, though? Bernadette says they're worried enough they're gonna head up to the cliffs.

MARILYN. Why?

ELAINE. Cos he goes up there a lot, apparently.

MAURICE. Really?

ELAINE. Yeah. *Too* often, apparently.

CIARAN. So you think he's gonna jump *off* them?

ELAINE. I don't know.

JANICE. He could be *any*where, Ma.

ELAINE. Which is why we should be out there helping them search.

MARILYN. Ma, we have to go.

ELAINE. Get the four o'clock boat.

MARILYN. I…

JANICE. We can't *do* the four o'clock boat.

MAURICE. Yeah, we have to head as well, actually.

ELAINE (*looks at him; beat*). What?! *Why?!*

MAURICE. Ah, we have our reasons.

FELIX. *Who* has to head?

HOLLY. *We* do.

FELIX. You and Maurice.

HOLLY. *And* you.

FELIX. Why do *I* have to go?

ELAINE (*to* MAURICE). Why do *you* have to go?

MAURICE. Ah, it's private, Ma. I don't wanna talk about it.

ELAINE. Jesus. (*Beat.*) Okay, well… *you* can stay till the four, though, can't you?

MAURICE. We actually can't, Ma, no.

ELAINE. Ah, you're joking! Why does everyone have to suddenly…? (*Beat.*) I mean…

FELIX. *I* can stay, Elaine.

ELAINE. Huh?

FELIX. *I* can stay and help look, if that's any use.

HOLLY. Da…

FELIX. There's Gina too…

HOLLY. Da, if *we're* going, *you're* going.

FELIX. Why?

HOLLY. Cos you're here as me and Maurice's guest. No one's gonna *want* you here without us.

FELIX. But...

HOLLY (*to the others*). Jesus, did that sound awful?

JANICE. Ma...

HOLLY. You know what I *mean*, though.

JANICE. Ma, you're okay with Felix staying, aren't you?

ELAINE. This is... (*Beat.*) There's a young man out there who...

MARILYN. He's fine.

ELAINE. ...who... You don't bloody *know* that, Marilyn! How can whether he lives or dies be of less value to you than getting on an earlier boat?

MARILYN. Because...

ELAINE. Jesus Christ!

MARILYN. Because I know it's an *act*, Ma.

ELAINE. No you don't.

MARILYN. Sure he's like the boy who cried wolf.

ELAINE. Except one day there *was* a fucking wolf...!

GINA (*entering from left; on 'fucking wolf'*). He wants me back!

ELAINE. What?!

MARILYN. Who?

GINA. Dave!

JANICE. Ah, Gina...!

GINA. I can't believe it!

MARILYN. And do *you* want *him* back?

GINA. *Yes*, are you joking?!!

JANICE. ...Ah, that's amazing!

GINA. He's heading to Dublin.

JANICE. When?

GINA. Today. He's getting the earliest flight he can and we're gonna meet tonight and have dinner, talk things through, he said should he get a hotel room somewhere fancy, and I said, 'Why not...?'

MARILYN. Wow.

GINA. '...Sure what can it hurt?' I mean, I know this whole thing has damaged some of the trust we have, and we'll have to work through that, I suppose, but still...

ELAINE. So...

GINA....you know?

ELAINE. So you're heading as well?

GINA. I have to, Elaine, I'm sorry. I need to get packed. I'm sorry, sis. Be happy for me.

She exits, left; pause.

MARILYN (*to* JANICE). Can you not get the four?!

JANICE. Can *you* not?

MARILYN. No.

JANICE. Well, neither can I.

MARILYN. Well, you'd better stay well away from us on the boat.

JANICE. *You'd* better stay well the fuck away from *us*. (*Beat.*) Fucking lowlife, you!

MARILYN. Fuck you!

JANICE. Fucking shit-stirrer.

She exits upstairs; pause.

MARILYN. Mam...

ELAINE *just shakes her head.*

CIARAN (*to* MARILYN). We'd better do the same.

MARILYN. Huh? Oh, right.

CIARAN. I'm sorry, Elaine.

He and MARILYN *head upstairs; pause.*

HOLLY. Dad...

FELIX. What.

HOLLY....the last thing Elaine's gonna need is you being a burden on her.

FELIX. Mm.

HOLLY. So you're coming with us, all right?

FELIX. Yeah.

HOLLY. Good. (*To* MAURICE.) We're gonna start getting packed, Maurice. (*Pause.*) Maurice...

MAURICE. Fine.

HOLLY. Come on, Da.

She and FELIX *head upstairs, leaving* ELAINE *and* MAURICE *alone. After several moments:*

MAURICE. Are you really that worried, Ma?

She nods.

Why?

ELAINE. Cos I know something's happened.

MAURICE. How?

ELAINE. I just do. It was the same with your da.

MAURICE. All right, well, look: I'll go *with* you, all right? Soon as everyone heads...

ELAINE. But you're heading too.

MAURICE. I'll, no, but I'll let them go ahead, and I can head back with you tomorrow.

ELAINE. You don't need to stay.

MAURICE. But I want to, and...

ELAINE. Maurice...

MAURICE. I do. I'm not gonna fucking *desert* you, Ma, when all this shit's going on.

ELAINE. Well, are you sure?

MAURICE. *Yes* I'm sure.

ELAINE (*beat*). All right, then. (*Beat*.) All right. Thanks, love. Why can't your sisters be like you?

MAURICE. Well, they have their *own* shit going on.

ELAINE. So responsible.

MAURICE. Stop.

ELAINE. So loving. You are. You're gonna be an *amazing* father, you know that? (*Pause*.) All right. I'm just gonna get my runners.

She exits, right. MAURICE sits down at the table. Pause. GINA enters from left, toothbrush in hand.

GINA. Nearly forgot to brush my teeth. (*Stops*.) You all right?

MAURICE. Yeah, of course.

GINA. You sure?

She goes to him, hugs him around the neck from behind.

*Some*times things go the way we want, am I right?

MAURICE. Exactly.

GINA. Not always but *some*times.

Beat. She kisses his cheek, exits upstairs. Silence. HOLLY comes down with her travelling bag. Pause.

HOLLY. Why aren't you packing?

ELAINE (*entering from right*). Where the hell did I put them?

She exits, left; pause.

HOLLY. Maurice...

MAURICE. I'm staying.

HOLLY. You what?

MAURICE. I'm gonna stay and help. My ma's on her own, so...

HOLLY. Right...

MAURICE....you know...

HOLLY. Yeah, but... (*Pause.*) Okay. (*Pause.*) Okay, well...

ELAINE (*entering again from left*). Have either of you seen my runners?

MAURICE. No.

HOLLY. No.

ELAINE. Jesus...

She exits upstairs.

HOLLY. Well, maybe me and my da'll stay as well.

MAURICE. Don't be stupid.

HOLLY. Why not? (*Pause.*) I mean, if they need as many people looking, you know, as they *say* they do, then...

MAURICE. Listen...

HOLLY. No, I'm gonna stay as well. (*To* FELIX, *who is now coming down the stairs with his travelling bag.*) All right, Dad?

FELIX. What?

HOLLY. You're happy to stay?

FELIX. Here?

HOLLY. Yeah, we're gonna help look for Aonghus.

FELIX. Oh. Uh... (*Beat.*) Okay. (*Beat.*) I might leave it to *you* lads to look, though, and just, whatever, hold down the fort...

HOLLY. All right.

FELIX.... have a beer or two, maybe. What time is it? Ah, maybe it's still a bit too early.

MAURICE (*to* ELAINE, *who is now coming down the stairs*). No sign?

ELAINE (*shakes her head; then*). *You* didn't see my runners, did you, Felix?

FELIX. No.

ELAINE. God's sake!

MAURICE. Well, look: maybe it's better if I head out ahead of you.

HOLLY (*to* MAURICE). Well, can I go with *you*?

ELAINE. Are you staying *too*, Holly?

HOLLY. Yeah.

ELAINE. Oh, *right*! Oh, well *that's* good.

HOLLY. Maurice…

ELAINE. That's *fantastic*, actually.

HOLLY (*pause*). Maurice…

MAURICE. Come *on*, then.

He heads for the door, then waits as she unplugs her phone.

ELAINE. Are you not gonna say goodbye to your sisters first?

MAURICE. We'll see them back in Dublin, Ma.

ELAINE. Yeah, but… (*To* GINA, *who enters from upstairs with her toothbrush.*) Maurice and Holly are staying.

GINA. Oh, are you?

HOLLY. Yeah, we're gonna help look for…

ELAINE (*to* HOLLY). Why the hell were you leaving in the *first* place?

MAURICE. Ma…

ELAINE. No that's fine. If it's private, it's private.

GINA. Right. Well I'll say goodbye to you *now*, then. (*Hugging* HOLLY.) It was lovely to meet you, Holly! You too, Felix. (*Hugging* MAURICE.) Take good care of her now, won't you.

MAURICE. Of course.

GINA. And congratulations again. (*Pause*.) All right. Listen, I still have some stuff to pack, so…

MAURICE. Go on.

HOLLY. Bye, Gina.

GINA. Bye.

She exits, left.

ELAINE (*to* MAURICE). So, which way are you gonna go?

MAURICE. I dunno.

ELAINE. To the cliffs?

HOLLY (*to* MAURICE). Well, if that's where everyone *else* is going, then maybe we should head in *another* direction.

MAURICE. Mm.

HOLLY. Just in case, like.

MAURICE (*to* ELAINE). I'll give you a shout when we decide.

ELAINE. All right. See you later, Holly.

MAURICE. See you, Ma.

He and HOLLY *leave. Pause.* FELIX *grabs one of Aonghus's books off the counter, sits down, starts leafing through it.* JANICE *and* STUART *come down the stairs with their travelling bags.*

JANICE. Least the water's calm today, Mam.

ELAINE. Mm.

JANICE. Listen, me and Stuart were wondering… and it's kind of embarrassing, but we just realised that you and the kids don't really see each other as much as you should.

ELAINE. We see each other.

JANICE. Yeah, but not that often.

ELAINE. I suppose.

JANICE. And never for more than, you know, a few hours at a time, and say no if you want to now, cos it may not be something that interests you, but if you wanted to take them at some point…

ELAINE. Take them.

STUART. Overnight, like.

JANICE. See, cos we never know if you'd *want* to.

ELAINE. Of course I would.

STUART. And we'd never want to presume, you know?

JANICE. And, of course, with Tom being as, uh…

ELAINE. *I* can handle Tom. I handled *you*.

JANICE. *I* wasn't that bad.

ELAINE. No you weren't. (*Beat.*) So, when would we do this?

JANICE. Well, you know we have Kelly's wedding…

ELAINE. Oh, right.

JANICE.… which, if we went, would mean staying over for maybe two nights.

ELAINE. *I* could do two nights.

JANICE. Could you do three?

ELAINE. Of course.

JANICE. Are you sure? It feels almost now like we're landing something on you.

ELAINE. Not at all.

STUART. Or taking advantage.

ELAINE. Why would it feel like that? (*Beat.*) I'd *love* to mind them. When is the date?

JANICE. The twenty-ninth. Like, less than a month.

ELAINE. Yeah, that's *completely* doable.

JANICE. Brilliant! I don't know why we haven't done this
    before! So weird. Anyway. We're gone. (*Hugging her.*) I love
    you, Ma.

ELAINE. You too. You don't mind me not walking you down.

JANICE. Of course not.

ELAINE. All right, bye.

JANICE. Bye.

STUART. Bye, Elaine.

    He hugs her. He and JANICE *go. After several moments:*

ELAINE. You all right, Felix?

FELIX (*still leafing through the book*). Yeah.

ELAINE. Can I get something for you? Or...

FELIX. No, I'm fine.

    She nods. GINA *enters from left with her travelling bag.*

GINA. Right. It was really great to see you, sis.

ELAINE. Yeah, you too.

    They hug.

GINA. I'm doing the right thing, amen't I?

ELAINE. Yes.

GINA. He'll be fine.

ELAINE. Who?

GINA (*meaning* AONGHUS). Your man.

ELAINE. Well...

GINA. He will. And let's chat next week, yeah? I'll fill you in
    on how everything's progressing.

ELAINE. Cool.

GINA. All right. Bye again, Felix.

FELIX. Bye.

GINA (*to* ELAINE). Bye.

ELAINE. Bye.

> GINA *goes. Pause.* FELIX *chuckles quietly to himself.*
>
> What is it?

FELIX. Ah, nothing. Just... (*Holds up Aonghus's book.*)

ELAINE. Right.

MARILYN (*appearing on the stairs with her travelling bag*). Are they gone? (*Beat.*) All right.

> *She comes down,* CIARAN *following.*
>
> So, we'll see you back home, Ma, yeah? (*Stops; pause.*) You not talking to me?

ELAINE. No.

MARILYN. Why not?

ELAINE. Because I don't want to, Marilyn.

MARILYN. You don't want to.

ELAINE. No.

MARILYN. Can I tell you something, Ma? For the last two years, I've really struggled with whether to say what I said last night, for fear of the damage it'd do...

ELAINE. It *did* do damage.

MARILYN. ... but also because I knew, if I didn't, then she wouldn't know it's something he's *capable* of. (*Beat.*) But it turns out I just made it up, is that right?

ELAINE. Marilyn...

MARILYN. That's what's been decided.

ELAINE. You *did* just make it up.

MARILYN. But why would I *do* that?

ELAINE. Just go, will you?

MARILYN. Tell me, though!

ELAINE (*exploding*). The same fucking reason you ever do *any*thing, Marilyn!! (*Beat.*) To make us all as miserable as *you* are!

MARILYN (*beat; then, through tears*). You're a fucking asshole, you know that?!

ELAINE. Am I.

MARILYN. Fucking dipshit!

ELAINE (*also through tears*). Well, you're a fucking *torment* and a *misery*!

MARILYN. Fuck you!

She exits.

ELAINE (*calling after her*)....Fucking bane of my fucking *existence*!!! (*Beat.*) I'm sorry, Ciaran.

He exits without acknowledging her.

Ciaran...! Oh, fuck you too! (*Slams the door.*) Jesus Christ!

She continues to cry. After several moments:

FELIX. You okay? (*Pause.*) You okay, Elaine?

ELAINE. I'm fine. Leave me alone.

FELIX. All right.

ELAINE. Go and have a fucking... *beer* or something.

Pause. He puts down Aonghus's book, rises, gets a beer from the fridge, goes outside. Pause. ELAINE goes upstairs. Silence. Then, from outside:

FELIX (*offstage*). How you doing, man?

AONGHUS (*offstage*). Hey.

He enters.

Hello? (*Pause.*) Hello? Marilyn? (*He goes back outside; offstage.*) Where is everybody?

FELIX (*offstage*). Gone.

AONGHUS (*offstage*). Where?

FELIX (*offstage*). Home. Except Maurice and... People are looking for you, you know.

AONGHUS (*offstage*). Home?!

FELIX (*offstage*) On the boat.

AONGHUS (*offstage*). Including Marilyn?

FELIX (*offstage*) Yeah, Elaine should be still in there.

AONGHUS (*offstage*) Did she know I'd disappeared?

FELIX (*offstage*) Elaine?

AONGHUS (*offstage*) No, Marilyn.

FELIX (*offstage*). Yeah, well, *all* of us did.

AONGHUS (*beat; entering again*). Elaine? (*Pause.*) Hello?

He sees his books piled up the counter, goes over, counts them, then looks at the one on the table.

(*To himself.*) Fucksake.

ELAINE (*coming down the stairs*). What are *you* doing here?

AONGHUS. She *left*?!

ELAINE. Who?

AONGHUS. Marilyn.

ELAINE. Where have you been?

AONGHUS. She *left*?!

ELAINE. Ciaran's mother passed away last night.

AONGHUS. Oh, Jesus...

ELAINE. Yeah, well...

AONGHUS. ...I'm sorry to hear that. (*Beat.*) And what about everyone else?

ELAINE. They had various things that came up. Maurice and Holly are here.

AONGHUS. Yeah, so, uh… thing said.

ELAINE. They're out looking for *you*.

AONGHUS. Well, at least *some*body gives a fuck.

ELAINE. *Every*one gives a fuck. They all think something awful's happened to you.

AONGHUS. Well, they're supposed to. (*Beat.*) Or Marilyn was. I thought, what a dope, I thought the worry of me maybe killing myself might make her realise how much I meant to her after all.

ELAINE. Aonghus…

AONGHUS. Yeah, I know.

ELAINE. She's moved on. People move on.

AONGHUS. *I* haven't.

ELAINE. I don't know what to say to you, Aonghus.

AONGHUS. And nobody even took a book, I see.

Pause. He sits down at the table. FELIX *enters, beer in one hand, a pair of women's runners in the other.*

FELIX. Is this them, Elaine?

ELAINE. Ah, where were they, Felix?

FELIX. Out under the bench.

ELAINE. Oh, for God's sake! Thank you. (*Takes them, starts putting them on.*) Does your mother know you're okay, Aonghus?

AONGHUS. Huh? No, not yet.

ELAINE. Well, will you ring her and *tell* her, then! (*As she finishes putting her runners on.*) What the hell am I…? (*Sighs.*)

AONGHUS. What.

ELAINE. I was putting them on to go out looking for *you*. (*Beat.*) Actually, *that's* what I'll do.

She rises.

AONGHUS. What?

ELAINE. Nothing.

She picks up the bucket of leftover food, heads to the front door, stops.

Call your mother, will you?

She exits.

FELIX. Where's she going?

AONGHUS. To feed the birds, I think.

FELIX. Oh.

AONGHUS *picks up his book, begins leafing through it.*

Very good.

AONGHUS. Hm? (*Then.*) Oh.

FELIX. That 'Fart' is good.

AONGHUS. Yeah, everyone seems to like 'Fart'.

FELIX. Do *you* not?

AONGHUS. No, I do. I like all of them.

FELIX. What's your favourite?

AONGHUS. Jesus... that's like asking a mother to pick her favourite *child*. (*Beat.*) Actually, hang on...

He looks for a poem, finds it; then, holding the page open as he hands it to FELIX.

That's a good one.

FELIX. Right. 'The Variables of Absence'.

AONGHUS. Mm.

FELIX *starts to read. After several moments:*

You *reading* it?!

FELIX. Yeah, is that not what you *want* me to do?

AONGHUS. Well, what*ever*, like.

FELIX *nods, resumes reading. After a moment,* AONGHUS *rises, wanders to the window, looks out.*

We begin to hear, in the distance, the sound of birds squawking.

That's her now. (*Beat; turning.*) Do you hear them?

FELIX, *still reading, doesn't respond.*

AONGHUS *turns back to the window.*

The sound of the birds gets louder and louder.

www.nickhernbooks.co.uk

facebook.com/nickhernbooks

twitter.com/nickhernbooks